About Island Press

Island Press is the only nonprofit organization in the United States whose principal purpose is the publication of books on environmental issues and natural resource management. We provide solutions-oriented information to professionals, public officials, business and community leaders, and concerned citizens who are shaping responses to environmental problems.

In 2004, Island Press celebrates its twentieth anniversary as the leading provider of timely and practical books that take a multidisciplinary approach to critical environmental concerns. Our growing list of titles reflects our commitment to bringing the best of an expanding body of literature to the environmental community throughout North America and the world.

Support for Island Press is provided by the Agua Fund, Brainerd Foundation, Geraldine R. Dodge Foundation, Doris Duke Charitable Foundation, Educational Foundation of America, The Ford Foundation, The George Gund Foundation, The William and Flora Hewlett Foundation, Henry Luce Foundation, The John D. and Catherine T. MacArthur Foundation, The Andrew W. Mellon Foundation, The Curtis and Edith Munson Foundation, National Environmental Trust, The New-Land Foundation, Oak Foundation, The Overbrook Foundation, The David and Lucile Packard Foundation, The Pew Charitable Trusts, The Rockefeller Foundation, The Winslow Foundation, and other generous donors.

The opinions expressed in this book are those of the author(s) and do not necessarily reflect the views of these foundations.

Saving the Ranch

SAVING THE RANCH

Conservation Easement Design in the American West

Anthony Anella and John B. Wright

PHOTOGRAPHS BY EDWARD RANNEY

ISLAND PRESS   Washington . Covelo . London

Copyright 2004 Anthony Anella and John B. Wright
Photographs Copyright 2004 Edward Ranney, both in book and in any publicity associated with it.

All rights reserved under International and Pan-American Copyright Conventions. No part of this book may be reproduced in any form or by any means without permission in writing from the publisher: Island Press, 1718 Connecticut Ave., Suite 300, NW, Washington, DC 20009.

Island Press is a trademark of The Center for Resource Economics.

Library of Congress Cataloging-in-Publication data.

Anella, Anthony.
Saving the ranch : conservation easement design in the American West / Anthony Anella and John B. Wright.
    p. cm.
Includes bibliographical references and index.
1.   Land use, Rural--Law and legislation--West (U.S.) 2.   Conservation easements--West (U.S.)   I. Wright, John B. (John Burghardt), 1950- II. Title.
KF5698.A77 2004
333.76'16'0978--dc22   2003024338

British Cataloguing-in-Publication data available.

Printed on recycled, acid-free paper

Design by Kristina Kachele
Manufactured in the United States of America

10 9 8 7 6 5 4 3 2 1

Frontispiece: Montosa Ranch near Magdalena, New Mexico (2003).

For Gibb, Kate, and Clare
A.A.

For Terry Jordan, Geographer
J.B.W.

Contents

Acknowledgments xi

Foreword LAWRENCE R. KUETER xiii

Preface xiv

Introduction 1

1. The Rancher's Choices 5
2. Conservation Easements 15
   Questions and Answers about Conservation Easements 30
3. Assembling Professional Advisers 41
4. The Baseline Report 51
5. Conservation Easement Design 61
6. Sieve Mapping 69
7. Conservation Development Design 83
8. Financial and Tax Advantages 97
9. Case Studies 107
10. Stewardship 137
11. Saving the Ranch 145

APPENDIX: *Model Deed of Conservation Easement* 147

Bibliography 163

About the Authors 164

Index 165

Acknowledgments

This book is inspired by B.W. and Billie Cox, the co-owners of the Montosa Ranch near Magdalena, New Mexico, and their tough-minded commitment to taking care of the land. The conservation of private land can be achieved only if landowners choose to care.

The McCune Charitable Foundation supported the publication of *Saving the Ranch* with enhanced production quality. This book began in 1995 as *The Open Lands Demonstration Project* with the support of the Graham Foundation for Advanced Studies in the Fine Arts, the Ucross Foundation, and the Koldyke Family Foundation. We are grateful to these foundations for their generous support.

We are also grateful to the following individuals: Edward Ranney, for his artistry as a photographer of the American landscape and for his integrity in standing by the project from its tentative early stages to the completion of this book; Tracy Conner, a Santa Fe attorney specializing in conservation easements, for her assistance with Chapter 8, "Financial and Tax Advantages," and for her review of the entire manuscript; Bruce Bugbee, for his tremendous knowledge of conservation easement design and his helpful advice on the manuscript; William Stockton, a journalist and a fourth-generation member of a Raton, New Mexico ranch family, for his advice on the manuscript and for sharing his insights on the economics of ranching; George Clark, a retired New Mexico banker, for his business integrity and for his love of the land; John Garrett, a distinguished California real estate attorney, for his trusted advice and encouragement; David Ater and Leon Mellow, Santa Fe realtors, for sharing their insights about real estate marketing; A. C. Taylor, an Albuquerque realtor specializing in ranch properties, for his skillful approach to innovation in real estate; Brian Panasiti, who provided invaluable help with the computer graphics, for his commitment to excellence; Teresa Bonner and Kristina Kachele, the book designers, for their talent and skill in making the book beautiful; and Heather Boyer, Anna Nunan, Jessica Poppe, and Christa Carignan of Island Press.

Anthony Anella
John B. Wright

Lake Valley Ranch near Hillsboro, New Mexico, as seen in the early years of its development (1998).

Foreword

I am writing this foreword after watching a television report describing the dramatic population growth for the United States that demographers believe will happen. It is impossible to listen to such a report without thinking about the consequences for the land and about the development pressures that such growth will place on the finite resource of land in the American West.

Representing and working with many landowners and agricultural land trusts over the last fifteen years have given me a unique view of private land conservation. I believe that if the great landscapes of the American West are protected, it will be done one property at a time. I also believe that it will be primarily by the private decisions of private landowners.

I think it would be wonderful if every ranch owner in the American West would read this book, not because a conservation easement is the appropriate decision for every ranch owner, but because development pressures and death and taxes are inevitable, and their impact will be worse for people who do not plan. This book is primarily about educating landowners about one of the choices available to them to be proactive about planning for these eventualities.

You cannot plan if you do not understand the choices available to you. *Saving the Ranch* describes, from a wonderful perspective, what a conservation easement can do for a landowner in the American West. Understanding this choice, and making a conscious decision about whether or not to protect the land, is something that every ranch owner should do.

Because placing a conservation easement to protect a ranch will be a decision that many landowners make, I do believe that we will still preserve much of the great landscapes of the American West, one property at a time. This book can help to make that happen.

Lawrence R. Kueter
Isaacson, Rosenbaum,
Woods & Levy, P.C.
Denver, Colorado

Preface

The American West is in conflict over the wise use of land. In fact, "wise use" means many different things to westerners. These points of view are based on a wide range of politics, science, and ideals. Environmentalists, seeing a diminishing of natural resources, say we need to preserve what is left. The most extreme even argue for an end to ranching. Land use planners try to zone property to keep it "scenic open space." Ranchers, seeing their livelihood threatened, say that neither preservation nor zoning compensates for lost grazing or development rights. Between these diverging points of view is a sensible center, a fair and market-driven way of conserving land.

Too often, opponents of ranching stress the overgrazing allowed by some ranch managers, while ignoring the good stewardship of most. Although we don't seek to romanticize ranching, we clearly don't agree with those who make blanket condemnations of it.

Ranches are worth saving. In addition to being a traditional and valued way of life in our country, competent cattle ranching makes elegant ecological sense. It is a sustainable, solar-powered system for producing food on arid and semi-arid land. Cattle ranching also protects open lands and supports wild animals. More than 75 percent of the West's winter range and migration corridors for wildlife are found on private land. National parks, forests, monuments, and wilderness areas are simply not sufficient to keep wildlife populations healthy. Wetlands, river corridors, ponds, lakes, historic sites, and scenic vistas are also found on private land. Yet ranchers are typically not compensated for providing many "conservation services"—those afforded by the sustainable production of cattle on grassland. We simply cannot afford to lose America's ranches.

Most Americans today are removed from earning their living on the land by four or five generations. As a result, we lose sight of our interdependence with the earth and forget how to sustain a balanced relationship with the land. In this regard there is a growing divide between the urban and rural points of view. Whatever your perspective about the proper balance between human beings and nature, the fate of ranches is strongly linked to the fate of the region. As the West grows, one thing unites us: a concern for the future of the land.

Land trusts, national conservation groups, certain agricultural organizations, and city/county open space programs are helping willing landowners keep their land from being extensively developed. A conservation easement that trades land protection for income tax benefits and estate tax benefits is often the tool to get this done. When you consider that most of the West's open space is ranchland and that ranch owners are an aging population increasingly concerned with estate planning, conservation easement becomes a potent and timely way of conserving land.

We wrote this book to provide ranchers and their advisers with a reliable, evenhanded explanation of what conservation easements are and how they work. Solid decisions are based on having solid information. We hope that *Saving the Ranch* forms a stronger bridge between ranchers and the various land conservation organizations across the West. The stakes are high. The legacy we leave to the next generation depends on it. Let's move forward with facts and mutual respect.

Pasture fences and Tres Montosas Mountain, Montosa Ranch.

Introduction

This book is based on a straightforward idea: a well-managed ranch is good for the land. The truth of this hinges on self-interest. Ranchers who carefully practice rotational grazing know that, by not doing so, they jeopardize their livelihood. It doesn't take long to wear out pastures. It is in a rancher's self-interest to manage the land in a sustainable way. If the realtor's mantra is "location, location, location," the rancher's is "stewardship, stewardship, stewardship." Take care of the land and the land will take care of you.

The biggest threat to ranching is conventional development—when the land ends up as a poorly planned subdivision. But, as the newcomers arrive, populations grow, and the demand for land in the West increases, how can any rancher stay in business when the financial rewards of subdividing are so high and the cattle prices are so low? That's a serious question. This book helps sort it out.

The success or failure of a cattle ranch is influenced by many variables, one of which is weather. Growing grass depends not only on the amount of rain, but on when it falls. There is a critical window during the growing season for rain to produce the most grass. And if the rain falls in the summer after a winter with little or no snowfall, the results can still be disappointing. The moisture delivered to the land as snowmelt seeps deep into the ground for an enduring benefit that allows the grass to take full advantage of the rains, when they come.

The changing demographics of this country also influence cattle ranching as an enterprise. As America becomes increasingly urbanized, political influence tilts away from the country. Grazing policies change based on the wishes of urban residents. The struggle to earn a living from the land becomes less understood. Ranchers are sometimes attacked as "fat cats" and "destroyers" of the West. Ranch families feel the strain as realtors watch from the sidelines, waiting for the call.

> I consider myself to be the luckiest person in the world to be able to live and work in God's creation on the Montosa Ranch. I want the ranch to be protected so that it looks like this for the next fifty generations and beyond. I want the land left as it is. I don't want to see the kind of subdivisions that are being developed around Datil on this land. I want other people to see that nature can be managed for the future, and that it doesn't have to be abused.
>
> —B. W. Cox, Rancher,
> Magdalena, New Mexico

The cattle market is another variable outside the rancher's control. Global free trade, the European Union's restrictions on importing American beef, and the power of meat packers with their captive supplies of feeder cattle all influence the price of steers. In a country inspired in part by the Jeffersonian ideal of the citizen-farmer, we have seen the individual family ranch give way to the economic efficiency of agribusiness.

The West is changing right before our eyes. There is no way to wish it away. It's time to move forward and take charge of what we can. As someone once said, you can't control the weather, but you can control what the weather does to you. But this is tough. How can ranchers possibly stay on the land with so many forces against them?

The answer for some people is a real estate tool called a conservation easement. A landowner can voluntarily donate some or all of the subdivision and development rights to a qualified agricultural organization or land trust and receive income tax and estate tax deductions. This is a way of claiming the financial benefits of conservation by leaving the ranch basically as is. A landowner can also use the income tax benefits of a donated conservation easement to offset the income received from selling some carefully sited lots. In both cases, the result can keep a ranch family on the land.

Conservation easement design offers a way to counterbalance the economic and demographic forces working against the rancher while protecting the land. This idea isn't new in the United States but is unfamiliar to many westerners. At first, a conservation easement may seem risky, but it is based on fact: how land is valued changes over time.

The story of a third generation New Mexico rancher illustrates the point. When his grandfather founded the family ranch, the land was valued based on its capacity to produce cattle. The land was viewed as a resource that allowed the production of this commodity. When his father took over the ranch, he found that selling hunting rights helped supplement his income from producing cattle. In addition to its commodity production value, the land had acquired a recreational value. Today, this third generation rancher has discovered that the land also has a *conservation* value. Like the recreational value, the conservation value can be used to supplement the income from producing cattle. By donating a conservation easement to a qualified group he trusted, the rancher claimed the financial benefits of this conservation value. Under the terms of the conservation easement, some lots can even be sold to raise cash as long as they don't destroy the land. That is what conservation easement design is all about: identifying and capturing the conservation value of the land for the benefit of the rancher while protecting the land by keeping most of the ranch open and in production. Conservation easements are a way of honoring and rewarding land stewardship.

The goal of this book is to show ranchers how to formalize their stewardship while capitalizing on the conservation value of the land. Lots of questions are raised and answered. How can land be appraised based on its potential for conservation? How can the rancher capitalize on this value? And how can conservation easement design help create this value?

Most ranchers are not interested in seeing their land subdivided. They value the land for the ranching way of life it provides. Most people buying land for a home are not interested in running a ranch. They value the land for the scenery, recreational opportunities, and privacy afforded by open space. Conservation easement design balances these two sides of the equation. On one side, it allows the land-rich and cash-poor rancher a way to get some equity out of the land while maintaining the viability of the land for agriculture. On the other side, it also protects the qualities of the land that make it attractive to conservation buyers. Conservation easement design is a way of putting the market to work for the rancher by capturing the economic value of conservation. It also puts the market to work for the land as an effective way of promoting—and financing—stewardship.

Ranchers must take care of their family's economic needs. This is hard-boiled reality. What follows is a different way of dealing with that reality. We will discuss a set of options ranging from "sell the place for development" to "put a conservation easement on the whole ranch." No judgments are made of whatever choice works for a family. But give conservation easement options a clear-eyed look. Ask tough questions. Demand straight answers. We believe conservation easement design can put the market to work in a positive way by financing the continued stewardship of western land by the people who know it best: ranchers.

Judge for yourself.

Looking south to Tres Montosas Mountain, Montosa Ranch.

The Rancher's Choices

At some time most ranch families must decide whether to stay in agriculture or to sell their land. This decision is often influenced by whether the next generation wants to continue ranching. Declining cattle prices, the increasing value of land for development, and other forces that are largely outside the family's control are also involved. There is a tipping point at which the weight of all these economic and personal considerations decides the future of a property (see Figure 1.1). That point is different in every case, and most families are used to thinking that they have only two choices—ranching or development. However, this book shows that options exist between the status quo and subdividing the whole ranch.

Once again, the goal of this book is to help conserve the integrity of ranchland and ranching as a way of life in the American West. It was written in response to certain economic and social realities that often lead the land-rich and cash-poor rancher to conclude that development is the only option for getting a lifetime of investment out of the land. However, this book does not promote development. Rather, it presents options so ranchers can make informed decisions about their future. The best way to maintain control of your destiny is to be clear about your goals and understand all your options. And the more options ranchers have, the better.

That's why this book was written primarily for ranchers. You are the audience we're talking to. However, land trust staff, lawyers, appraisers, accountants, realtors, developers, conservationists, and the general public may find value here as well. Conservation easements are a subject worth knowing for many westerners.

All options discussed in this book respect private property rights. Making solid decisions about the land you own is the key to controlling your future. To do this, you have to ask some tough questions: If your children inherited your ranch today, what would the tax bill be? How

KEEP THE RANCH	SELL THE RANCH
Personal ethics and values	Conflicts with newcomers
Profit—livestock, crops	Lack of profit—livestock, crops
Minimal or no debt	Debt
Payment for "ecological services"	Negative public perception of ranching
Cropland Reserve Program	Regulations on land use, grazing, biocides
Wetland Reserve Program	Droughts, pests, disease
Forest management income	Lack of forest
Town income	Isolation, lack of town jobs
Ample water	Water supply problems
New crops	Failed promise of new crops
Eco-tourism income	Grazing lease fees rise
Specialty meat	Predation
Wildlife income	Endangered species conflicts
Love of way of life	Family issues—frustration with way of life
Partial development income	All or nothing—either ranch or subdivide

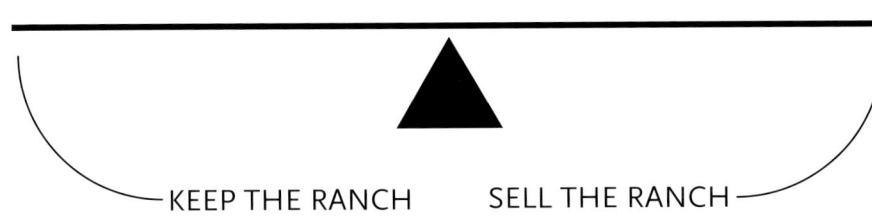

Figure 1.1 | Tipping Point

would it be paid? Who will manage your ranch after you are gone? What do you want your ranch to look like a hundred years from now? Your answers to these questions are personal and private; they are between you and your family. But now there are allies in agricultural organizations and land trusts that can help you achieve your goals.

One of the greatest threats to keeping a ranch in the family is the estate tax. Federal and state estate taxes combined can be as high as 55 percent of a ranch's fair market value, a fact that can force heirs to sell all or part of the property to pay the bill. A lack of estate planning is often a real problem in ranch country. But what if a way existed to keep the ranch in the family by reducing or eliminating the estate tax burden and by creating more income possibilities to pay off debt? This book shows how ranchers can reduce estate taxes, generate and shelter income, and combine land conservation with estate planning.

Conservation easements are a big part of this. This tool is a voluntary legal agreement between a landowner and a land trust or other qualified group that permanently protects the conservation values of a ranch by limiting or restricting future development. The financial advantages of a conservation easement include potential income tax deductions as well as reduced estate and, in some cases, property taxes. These issues are discussed in the following chapters.

It is important to note that a conservation easement leaves the land in *private ownership.* You continue to own and use your land for ranching, or you can sell it, or you can pass it on to your heirs.

The range of ranchers' choices is amazing. The "decision tree" shown in Figure 1.2 reveals the flexibility of conservation easements in meeting a wide range of financial and personal needs. For example, if you choose to sell the ranch, there are many options. Each involves individual values. If you are primarily interested in getting as much money out of the land as possible, you can subdivide the ranch into as many lots as possible. You can do this yourself, or you can sell your land to a conventional developer who will subdivide it for you. If you prefer

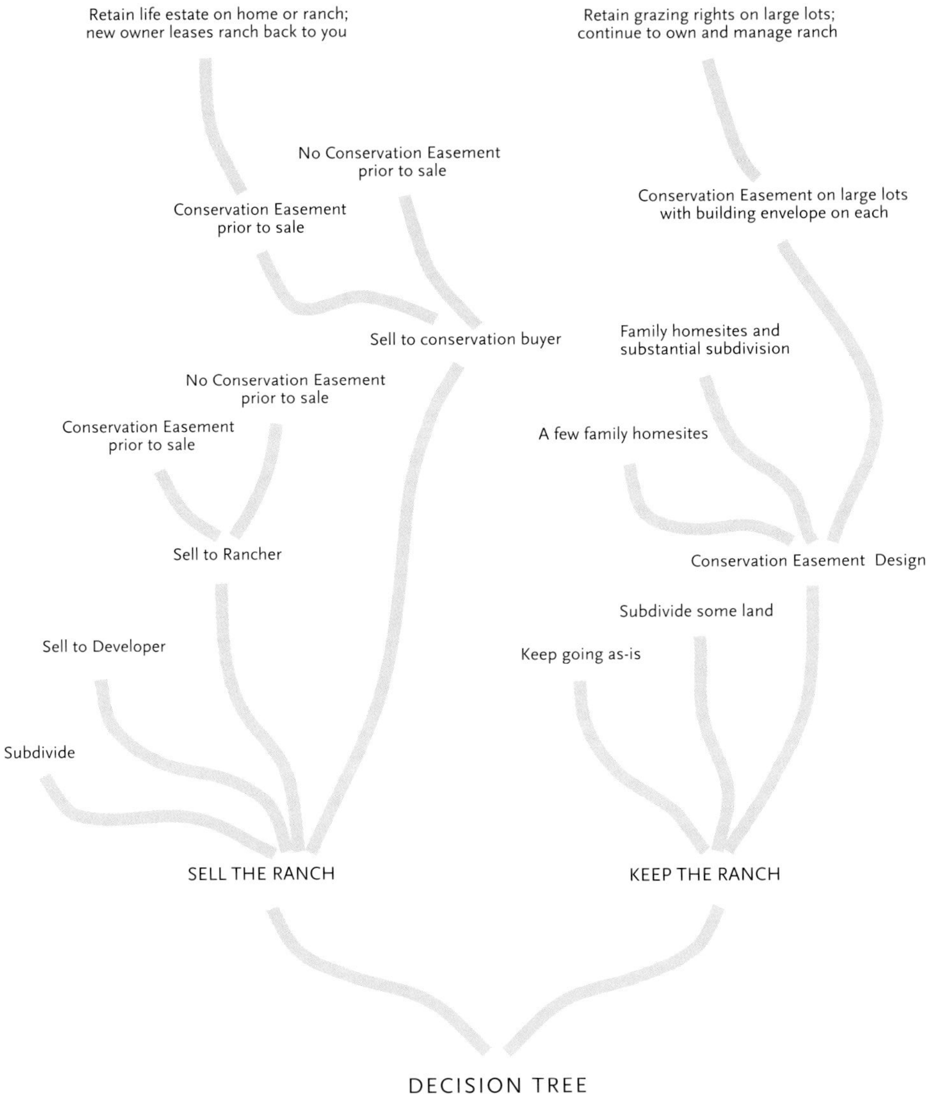

Retain life estate on home or ranch; new owner leases ranch back to you

Retain grazing rights on large lots; continue to own and manage ranch

No Conservation Easement prior to sale

Conservation Easement on large lots with building envelope on each

Conservation Easement prior to sale

Sell to conservation buyer

Family homesites and substantial subdivision

No Conservation Easement prior to sale

A few family homesites

Conservation Easement prior to sale

Sell to Rancher

Conservation Easement Design

Subdivide some land

Sell to Developer

Keep going as-is

Subdivide

SELL THE RANCH

KEEP THE RANCH

Figure 1.2 | Decision Tree

DECISION TREE

to see your land stay in ranching forever, you can place a conservation easement on it and then sell it to another rancher or a "conservation buyer" who is interested in the beauty of the place. If you sell your ranch with no conservation easement on it—even to another rancher—you run the risk of the land being subdivided in the future. The most obvious disadvantage of selling the ranch is losing control of the land.

If you choose to keep the ranch, you also have several choices. You can keep going as is or subdivide some land—based on either a conventional or a conservation development pattern. If you need to get some money out of the land but do not want to see your land heavily subdivided, you can place a conservation easement on the land while retaining limited development rights. These limited development rights can range from a few family homesites to multiple large lots with designated building envelopes. In both cases you can choose to retain the grazing rights. Various hybrids of development can be designed to meet your financial goals while protecting your land and retaining your control over ranch management.

The decision tree illustrates how conservation easements create options. The landowner can receive easement benefits whether he or she decides to keep or sell the ranch, or adopts the middle ground approach of a limited, protective development.

Conservation easement design works by putting the market to work for the rancher by capturing the value of conservation as a commodity. *This is true whether you choose to develop all, part, or none of the ranch*. For example, if you decide you want to keep your ranch just like it is, the ranch still has a built-in development value. Population pressure will only increase this value. Usually, unless you develop your land, you will not be able to capture this value. The one exception is a conservation easement. A conservation easement can be either donated to or purchased by a conservation organization such as a land trust. If you donate a conservation easement, you are "paid" in reduced estate and income taxes based on the value of the donation. If you sell a conservation easement on your land (also called "Purchase of Development Rights" or PDR), you are paid with cash. The problem with a PDR is that very few conservation groups have that kind of cash. In contrast, the estate tax reduction works for any ranchers who own their land. The income tax deduction works best for ranchers with significant income to shelter from the sale of land or other sources (see Chapter 8).

All this can be confusing for ranchers who are used to valuing land based on its capacity to produce cattle. It can also be confusing for the developer who is used to seeing land only as a marketable commodity. In addition to the "commodity-production" and "residential" value, land has a "conservation" value. But how is this conservation value appraised? How can ranchers capitalize on it? How can land developers factor it into their projects? And how can conservation easement design help create this value while protecting the land?

The following chapters deal with these questions and more. In short, conservation easements provide financial and emotional rewards for stewardship. This is fundamentally different from conventional development—all those small lots covering ranchland all over the West.

Conventional Development

Conventional development refers to subdivisions where all the land is divided into lots and roads with the only open space being steep slopes, floodplains, and arroyos. This approach views land as a commodity to be exploited. It is based on the "residential" value of property, and is often speculative and driven by the lending habits of financial institutions and the need to service debt.

"Success" is the short-term conversion of land into cash. This is often accomplished by minimizing infrastructure costs. Ironically, this pattern of development can also minimize the value of the developed land in the marketplace. It can also diminish the value of the land as an attractive, long-term investment.

Conventional development is based on a two-step design process. First, lay out the roads with the least cost by avoiding steep slopes. Such roads commonly parallel creeks, intrude on wildlife habitats, and cross productive rangelands. Second, subdivide the land into lots. Here is where the cost-savings can break down. The simple design goal is to maximize the number of lots based on the zoning code, or—where no zoning code is enforced—to subdivide the land into parcels the developer can sell quickly. The resulting lot lines cross topographic features such as steep slopes as if they weren't there. Indeed, for the surveyor sitting in front of his computer back at the office, they aren't there. The contours are a mere abstraction. The final product is an artless connect-the-dots (in this case, connect-the-roads) plat that ignores the potential to create real value by protecting the productivity and beauty of the land. The first few lots may fulfill the marketing promise of privacy and seclusion in a spacious country setting, but by the time the last lots are sold—if they can be sold—this promise is broken.

In southern Colorado, a division of *Forbes* magazine has developed the historic Trinchera Ranch into a vast subdivision. According to a marketing brochure, the "guaranteed minimum size of each ranch site is five acres" and the terms are "exceptionally easy." What makes the terms exceptionally easy is that only land is being sold. No electricity. No phone. No water. Just land. Even the access roads are dirt.

The Trinchera development began in 1972. To promote sales the developer used an interesting marketing argument:

> It's no secret that the world's population is expected to double by the turn of the century. It doesn't take much imagination to realize how this people-boom will affect the reserves of available land in the United States.
>
> A Sangre de Cristo Ranch is your opportunity to purchase five magnificent acres of America's dwindling real estate for yourself and for the future of your loved ones. Equal in size to twenty city lots, five acres contains 217,800 square feet of land.

That sounds like a lot of land to a newcomer. Never mind the fact that each 217,800-square-foot lot is surrounded by a cookie-cutter pattern of other 217,800-square-foot lots. The development has transformed some of the most beautiful ranch country in America into a suburb.

In southwestern New Mexico the developers of the "Wild Horse Ranch" offer parcels of 20+ acres in a "spacious country setting." "Enjoy lots of elbow room on your very own piece of land," says the brochure. "Nature is your backyard!" Never mind that your backyard is also your neighbor's backyard. What is being sold is a lifestyle myth. The cartoon-like names of the roads—Stallion Circle, Buckskin Trail, Round-up Road, Bronco Lane—complete the conversion of the ranching landscape into a residential area.

Conservation Easements and Limited Development

Conservation easement design ranges from protecting the entire ranch to creating a limited, protective development. (This is explained in more detail in the following chapters.) In all cases, conservation easement design is based on protecting ranchland as a natural resource. "Success" is the long-term stewardship of the earth, which translates into the appreciation of land value over time. It honors one of America's great strengths—private property rights—while respecting the rights of future generations.

Conservation easement design recognizes that some land is suitable for conservation and some is more appropriate for residential development. Conventional development rarely makes this distinction. It treats all land the same without regard to the destruction of ranches, watersheds, and wildlife habitats. Conservation easement design is site-specific and promotes the stewardship of natural resources.

What truly defines conservation easement design is love for the land—not a concept that "pencils out" at first glance. It should be said plainly: The main reason people place a conservation easement on a ranch comes from the heart. They do it because they can't bear the thought of the place being covered with houses.

Ranchers who want to get as much money as possible out of the land should probably subdivide their place into "ranchettes." This is the conventional approach to the development of rural land. There is a much larger market of people who can afford to buy twenty to thirty acres at $19,900 than people who can afford to pay for a carefully designed protective development. However, you get what you pay for. You also get what you sell for. Lots in protective developments often sell for more per acre than conventional lots. Always "run the numbers" and compare the trade-offs. But, if ranchers do not want to see their land completely subdivided, they should consider a conservation easement design.

Getting It Done on the Ground

Conservation easement design offers a way to counterbalance the economic forces that threaten the existence of ranching as a viable way of life. It recognizes the contribution to stewardship that ranchers make and allows them to capitalize on this contribution. It does this by reducing or eliminating the estate tax burden, and by creating more income possibilities through limited development, allowing a family to pay off debt while preserving the integrity of the land.

Conservation easement design is one of the last best chances for ranchers to maintain their way of life. But getting it done on the ground is what matters. The following chapters show how.

Grama grass and Piñon-Juniper savannah, Montosa Ranch.

2 Conservation Easements

First, a legal definition: A conservation easement is a legal interest in private land that perpetually limits development in order to protect significant agricultural, scenic, ecological, and historic resources. Conservation easements are voluntarily donated or sold by a landowner to a qualified conservation organization such as a land trust. When a conservation easement is donated, federal income and estate tax deduction possibilities exist similar to those that may result from making a contribution to a church or charity (see Chapter 8). Conservation easements have also been called scenic easements, agricultural conservation easements, open space easements, historic preservation easements, and conservation restrictions.

Now, in plain English: A conservation easement is a family decision to save your ranch and leave a legacy of good land. With a conservation easement you donate or sell all or most of your development rights to an organization you trust in order to protect specified conservation values. When the conservation easement is conveyed to the land trust and the easement deed is recorded, these development rights are extinguished. The land trust cannot itself use them, or sell them. They are gone for all time. The donation is forever, but *you still own your land* and can ranch it, sell it, lease it, or give it to your children. The group you donate or sell the easement to watches over your place, even after your death, and makes sure that no future landowner violates your vision of how the land should be used. The public need not be granted access to the place. The easement is forever and runs with the land. A conservation easement is basically a formal declaration of long-term stewardship.

It is worth saying again: The conservation easement donor still owns the land and continues to use it for ranching and for the amount of development agreed to in the easement document.

The land trust or other easement holder is an ally who shares your vision of how you want your land managed for the future. It is legally and morally bound to defend your land against harm forever.

Private Property Rights

Conservation easements fully respect private property rights. In fact, the tool is a powerful way of helping landowners do what they want with their land.

Fundamental to the American idea of property ownership is the concept of fee simple title. A landowner is vested with all necessary rights to treat land as a fully marketable commodity. These rights can be imagined as a bundle of sticks. Any stick—water rights, mineral rights, timber rights, development rights—can be separated and legally sold, leased, traded, or otherwise conveyed in the marketplace. Those interests in land, along with such things as utility and road easements, are "positive" in the sense that they grant someone else the right to do something.

Landowners also have the legal right to conserve their land by restricting housing development, mining, and timber harvesting. This is done through a conservation easement that is donated or sold to a qualified conservation entity. In a conservation easement certain rights are transferred with the remainder retained. Each project is individually designed to meet the needs of the landowner, the limits of the land, and the goals of the land trust. Conservation easements are "negative" only in the sense that they keep something from happening on a piece of land in the future, something the landowner does not want to happen.

Conservation easements are not about losing control of your land. They are about controlling what happens to it.

Legal Basis

Conservation easements have been used for decades in America. More than 7,500 conservation easements exist nationwide, protecting more than 4 million acres of agricultural land, wildlife habitat, historic sites, and open space. The use of conservation easements has increased largely because landowners are interested in seeing their land protected. Certain laws have been passed to help.

The legal basis for easements comes from three sources: common law, federal law, and state law. English common law is the legal foundation of private property rights and right-of-way concepts. Conservation easements were permitted for decades based on this common law authority. The Tax Reform Act of 1976 and the Tax Treatment Extension Act of 1980 were the first specific federal statutes. Section 170(h) of the Internal Revenue Code was drafted to provide guidance on qualifying land for federal tax benefits for easement donation. Land must contain "significant conservation values" such as ecological, open space (including agricultural land), historic, and recreation resources. All open space including agricultural lands qualifies if it has been identified "pursuant to a clearly delineated Federal, State, or local governmental conservation policy." In 1981, the Uniform Conservation Easement Act brought more legal consistency to the technique. This act served as the legal foundation for the majority of state statutes enabling conservation easements. Each state law differs in certain administrative technicalities, but all fifty states except Wyoming recognize the right of landowners to donate easements.

Land Trusts and Conservation Easements

A land trust is a private, nonprofit conservation organization that uses voluntary methods to protect open landscapes. Trusts are not government regulatory agencies. They are a grassroots expression of people's dedication to protect ranches, farms, and other undeveloped lands.

Conservation easements are routinely received by land trusts and national conservation organizations. Land purchases, purchase of development rights, land exchanges, and other devices are also employed. All of these tools are voluntary and financially compensate the landowner—a direct contrast with government regulatory systems of land use control.

The first systematic use of conservation easements occurred along the Blue Ridge and Natchez Trace parkways in the 1930s. By the 1950s, easements were being used on farmland along Wisconsin's Great River Road. In the 1960s, easements were employed in Idaho's Sawtooth National Recreation Area and on ranches. The tremendous expansion in local land trusts since then has greatly increased their use throughout the United States.

Land trusts originated in 1890 with the Trustees of Reservations in Massachusetts. By 1950, there were 53 land trusts, primarily in New England. Fifteen years later, land trusts totaled more than 130. In 1981, 431 trusts were scattered all over the country. Among the first groups in the West were the Montana Land Reliance, Jackson Hole Land Trust, and Colorado Open Lands. As of 2003, more than 1,200 local and regional land trusts were operating in all fifty states—protecting over 2 million acres. The use of conservation easements by land trusts increased 475 percent from 1990 to 2000.

The missions of land trusts vary. National groups like the Rocky Mountain Elk Foundation focus on big game habitat. The American Farmland Trust works to keep farms and ranches undeveloped and in production. The Nature Conservancy specializes in securing habitats for rare species. The Trust for Public Land engages in cooperative projects with local groups to protect important open space.

Local and regional trusts in the West are increasing in number and effectiveness.

The Montana Land Reliance holds 515 easements on more than 500,000 acres of ranchland—an unrivaled record of accomplishment. The Taos Land Trust holds some 40 easements in a rapidly developing region of New Mexico. Up and down the spine of the continent, more than 60 land trusts are working with their neighbors to keep local landscapes intact.

Ponderosa Pine, Piñon, and Juniper growth, Montosa Ranch.

Agricultural organizations have also joined the effort. The Colorado Cattlemen's Agricultural Land Trust has worked with ranchers to place easements on over 152,000 acres in just a few years. Stockgrower organizations in Wyoming, Nevada, Arizona, and California have followed suit. The National Cattlemen's Beef Association has endorsed conservation easements and the purchase of development rights as effective programs for keeping ranches in production.

The Conservation Easement Process

The completion of a conservation easement involves eleven basic steps. While these steps are presented in their most logical order, events often dictate some variation. What should never vary are three basic rules: Get professional advice, run the numbers, and trust your instincts.

Step 1: Initial Meeting between Landowner and Land Trust
The landowner and land trust personnel tour the ranch. It is a chance to discuss the general qualifications of the land for easement protection, identify the mission of the land trust, and determine the basic goals of the landowner. When selecting a land trust it is important for you to find the right match between your interests as a rancher and the interests of the land trust. Chapter 3 includes advice on selecting a land trust.

Step 2: Landowner Consults Professional Advisers
A conservation easement restricts the use of land forever. It should not be entered into lightly. Lawyers and accountants may or may not be informed about conservation easements, and some react negatively to the idea until they learn more. Land trusts have the names of advisers with experience. Get the facts before going too far into the process. Chapter 3 includes advice on assembling professional advisers. It is best to reach a basic understanding of typi-

cal easement restrictions at this point, and to then let the design process and negotiations work out the specifics.

Step 3: Land Title Information

A title company prepares an up-to-date title report. This will verify the legal ownership of the property and determine whether mortgages or liens exist that might extinguish the easement if there were a foreclosure. If a mortgage exists, the lender must "subordinate" its lien to the lien of the easement. This is commonly done if the numbers are right. If $1 million is owed by the landowners and the easement would reduce the paper value of a ranch to $700,000, the lender would not agree to subordinate because its loan would not be fully secured. If it appears that the easement will not jeopardize the lender's interest (that is, the "after" value of the land exceeds the outstanding loan balance), the project may proceed, but the lender must sign a formal "subordination agreement" once the easement appraisal is completed. The title report also determines the ownership of mineral rights and is used to prepare an accurate map of the property. This map is essential for preparing the baseline report and designing easement restrictions.

Step 4: Baseline Report Preparation

A consultant or land trust staff prepares a baseline report of the property (see Chapter 4). This report has four major purposes:

1. Qualify the property for federal and state tax deductions for an easement donation.
2. Locate significant conservation values to design an effective conservation easement.
3. Describe ranch improvements and the condition of the property at the time of the easement gift. This will form the basis for easement monitoring and enforcement.
4. Provide a clear basis for continued land stewardship.

For a conservation easement to be a "qualified conservation contribution" a real property interest must be donated in perpetuity to a tax-exempt land trust or other eligible organization for conservation purposes. Federal law and Section 170(h)(4)(A) of the Internal Revenue Code describe four qualification categories of "conservation purposes":

1. "The preservation of land areas for outdoor recreation by, or the education of, the general public."

The recreation provision is rarely used because most landowners do not want to grant public access. The education portion is sometimes used where environmental field trips, nature study, and other learning experiences are part of the easement design.

2. "The protection of a relatively natural habitat of fish, wildlife, or plants, or similar ecosystems."

Most ranches qualify under this provision because they contain wildlife habitats, rangelands, forests, creeks, and other natural resources. The existence of threatened or endangered species on the ranch helps qualify the property for tax deductions, but does not single out the landowner for additional federal regulations. In fact, unless the landowner does a "Habitat Protection Plan" or receives direct cash payments as part of the Wetland Reserve Program (WRP) or Cropland Reserve Program (CRP), the federal government is not involved except to grant routine tax deductions. An easement often takes the pressure off landowners because their ranch management is compatible with the survival of the species and they have voluntarily kept development off the critical habitat.

3. "The preservation of open space (including ranches and forests) where such preservation is (1) for the scenic enjoyment of the general public, or, (2) is pursuant to a clearly delineated Federal, State, or local governmental conservation policy, and will yield a significant public benefit."

This purpose is the most widely used and diverse of all four categories. For "scenic" open space, *visual* and not physical access is required from a public road, waterway, or adjacent public land. The public needs only to see the land, not walk on it. Scenic By-Ways, river corridors, parks, and Wilderness Areas help ranches qualify by supporting these open space resources. "Non-scenic" open space also qualifies, such as groundwater recharge areas, airport noise buffers, and ranchland far from sight. Such areas and more can be deemed important in a government policy such as the Farmland Protection Act, the local Conservation District Plan, or a local county comprehensive or open space plan. Open space qualification is generally straightforward.

4. "The preservation of an historically important land area or a certified historic structure that is listed in the National Register, or is located in a registered historic district."

Land that contributes to the integrity of an historic site such as a battlefield or a structure on the National Register of Historic Places would qualify. The records of the State Historic Preservation Office (SHPO) help in assessing a property. The presence of an historic structure does not mandate protection unless cash payments are received to restore the building. The easement does not require a landowner to fix up an old building or maintain it. The land trust will seek a restriction on it being bulldozed. Archaeological resources, ranging from a scatter of arrowheads to dwelling sites, help qualify a property, but generally do not mean a change in ranch management.

A baseline report—the systematic assembly of data on the characteristics and condition of the property—is the document that qualifies a donated conservation easement for tax benefits. It is also used to design the conservation easement restrictions and monitor the enforcement of these restrictions. Fieldwork, research, and interviews with the landowner and other experts result in the creation of vegetation and landform maps, wildlife lists, and inventories of existing structures and improvements.

The baseline report also establishes permanent, easily relocated photo points for documenting and monitoring the initial baseline conditions. A clear statement of the property's qualifications for conservation easement tax benefits is included. While a conservation easement needs to fulfill only one of the four criteria listed above, the baseline report must identify all values found on the property. The standard is not met if significant conservation values are left unprotected.

If the landowner does not own all the mineral rights, a geologist must evaluate the potential for commercial mineral deposits being found and exploited on the ranch. If none exist, the geologist writes a letter indicating that the likelihood of commercial minerals (or future surface mining) is so remote as to be negligible. In most cases, ranches meet the so-called Remoteness Test because either no minerals are present or the cost of extracting them makes mining commercially infeasible. If commercial deposits do exist as well as a good chance they will be developed, the property would probably not qualify for tax deductions from the easement gift. This does not apply to oil and gas deposits. Some land trusts will accept easements with a commercial oil field in place because this helps the rancher financially. Other trusts may walk away.

The baseline report should be clearly written. One of its main functions is to assure that monitoring of the land for easement violations is easily done. This protects the landowner against frivolous enforcement actions and protects the land from violations of easement terms.

Step 5: Assess Need for Limited Development

The landowner and his or her advisers determine if income is needed from selling some lots. A conservation easement results in an income tax deduction useful to the donor only if there is income to shelter.

If development is needed to generate income, both a standard baseline report and a more detailed analysis of the land will be needed. Chapters 6 and 7 explain the steps involved. Such projects are much more complex and time-consuming than a simple easement where homesites are reserved for family members. Some land trusts may decide not to work on projects with a significant development component. In such cases, an easement receiver experienced in more complicated deals must be found.

Step 6: Negotiate Easement Restrictions

Creating a viable easement is the central goal (see Chapter 5). A "Deed of Conservation Easement" declares the basic goals of the project, then spells out "Consistent" and "Inconsistent" uses of the property. When writing this deed, certain rights are voluntarily severed from the underlying ownership. These rights are donated to a qualified group and extinguished when the easement is recorded.

Negotiating restrictions involves compromise, but each side may have certain bottom-line requirements. The rancher may want to retain the right to build a few houses for family members or even subdivide a portion of the place to make the easement donation possible. Easement receivers generally want to minimize future development. This apparent conflict can be resolved, however, if new structures can be located off of key habitats and away from scenic vistas. Successful negotiations result in many mutually satisfying agreements.

Easement restrictions usually focus on basic land uses and avoid everyday ranch management. The easement must allow new agricultural practices that support basic stewardship goals. Since the easement document is permanent, the following land uses must be addressed with care: subdivision, houses, roads, timber management, minerals, water, commercial–industrial development, signs, telecommunications towers, gravel pits, waste disposal, recreational use, motorized recreational vehicles, feedlots, guest ranching, and hunting. Any possible future use may be discussed during negotiations.

Step 7: Easement Appraisal and Financial Analysis

The landowner hires an independent, certified land appraiser to determine the monetary value of the development rights to be donated. The appraiser must have experience with conservation easements. Land trusts have lists of suitable professionals. Chapter 3 offers advice on selecting an appraiser. Chapter 8 covers financial and tax matters.

The appraisal of conservation easements is a three-step process. The first step is to conduct a "before" appraisal. In this step the property is valued "as is" based on its highest and best use—*before* a conservation easement is placed on it. The "highest and best use" is typically residential development. Comparable sales of similar properties are used in this calculation. The before value reflects the fee simple interest in property as a complete bundle of rights—including the right to subdivide and develop.

The next step is to conduct an "after" appraisal. In this step the property is valued as if *after* the conservation easement restrictions are in force. The fair market value of the conservation easement for tax deduction purposes is determined by subtracting the after value from the before value.

The percentage of reduction in value—or "takedown"—varies widely depending on the intensity of land development pressure in the area and the restrictiveness of the easement. For areas with tremendous subdivision activity, the takedown could be 70 percent or more. For remote areas with slight development pressure, the easement may not cause substantial reduction in the land's market value. In the West, takedowns of 30–50 percent are typical, but a full appraisal is the only reliable way of knowing.

A third step comes up in projects where the landowner holds adjacent land out of the easement or sells lots next door. In these cases, the appraiser must determine the "enhancement value" that results from the existence of the conservation easement. The enhancement value derives from the fact that land adjacent to protected land becomes more valuable than land adjacent to unprotected land. If the market price of adjacent land owned by the donor or any land owned by the landowner or related parties is increased because of the presence of the easement, this amount must be subtracted from the value of the easement. The Internal Revenue Service (IRS) requires an accounting of any added value. The enhancement value should be carefully considered when analyzing the financial implications of any conservation easement transaction—*especially one with a development component.*

Regarding conservation easement donations, there is a simple rule: Always run the numbers.

Some landowners choose to have a preliminary appraisal prepared. This gives a rough idea of the value of the contribution and allows better estate and tax planning calculations. Keep in mind that a final appraisal has a short shelf life. A conservation easement must be recorded within sixty days of the official date of the appraisal for the donor to be in compliance with the IRS rules. However, it is possible to get a certified update if the easement process gets slowed down for some reason.

Overaggressive appraisals are a sure "red flag" with the IRS. The IRS has been less concerned with the qualification of ranches than with *how much* is being claimed in tax benefits. The best policy is fairness and the use of an experienced, certified appraiser.

Step 8: Finalize Easement Design

Once the baseline report is completed, the easement deed is drafted, the appraisal is prepared, and the tax and financial implications are known, the easement design is finalized. It may be necessary to reword certain restrictions, relocate "building envelopes" or lots, add or subtract lots, and recalculate tax and income figures. This is the time to consider the transaction carefully to make sure it achieves the landowner's goals while still protecting the land.

Step 9: Present Easement to Land Trust Board

The land trust board formally reviews the proposed conservation easement. Staff and board members may want to visit the property for a tour. Their review can take a few weeks or several months depending on the project's complexity. Never assume an easement will be accepted "as is" or quickly.

Land trusts will ask for a "stewardship endowment contribution." This money is essential for land trusts to conduct annual monitoring visits, pay for staff time, and create a legal defense fund for enforcing the easement. In the event a future landowner violates your easement, the trust must have the resources to pay the legal fees to defend it. A typical endowment contribution is about $5,000–$10,000 for a simple easement and $20,000 or more for complex projects with lot sales as part of the design. Such contributions are negotiable and tax deductible. Some trusts may waive the contribution in cases where a landowner does not have the ability to pay. However, the contribution is typically required. It is a vital part of the easement process because it gives the land trust the funds it needs to monitor the land and defend the easement. It takes money to honor the wishes of landowners forever.

Step 10: Record the Conservation Easement

Once the land trust board votes to accept the easement, they and the donor sign the deed. The landowner then files the deed in the county courthouse. For tax purposes the donation officially occurs when the conservation easement is recorded. Filing on December 31 places the easement donation in that calendar year for tax purposes. Carefully consider the timing of the recording with the help of your financial and legal advisers. If the gift is planned to offset income from the sale of lots, then the recording should be timed to coincide with the sale of the first lot in order to maximize the tax benefits. An escrow agent can be used to facilitate this. See Chapter 8 for more information on the financial and tax implications of donating a conservation easement.

Montosa Ranch.

Step 11: Stewardship

The landowner and all subsequent owners are legally bound to honor the easement. The land trust monitors the land, generally once a year, to assure that violations have not occurred (see Chapter 10). However, landowners are the true stewards of their property.

Questions and Answers about Conservation Easements

Why donate a conservation easement?

To keep land available for ranching, to keep it in the family, to accomplish estate planning goals, to protect the land's beauty and wildlife habitat, and to keep the ranch from being converted to intensive development. There are potential estate, income, and other tax benefits, which may provide financial incentives, but most people donate a conservation easement because they love their land.

How common are conservation easements?

Over 7,500 conservation easements exist in the United States covering about 4 million acres. The tool has existed since the 1890s and has been used routinely since the 1960s.

Who is in favor of conservation easements?

The National Cattlemen's Beef Association, American Farmland Federation, American Farmland Trust, Wyoming Stockgrower's Association, Colorado Cattlemen's Association, Nevada Stockgrower's Association, California Cattlemen's Association, and over 1,200 land trusts nationwide. Many land trusts have the mission of conserving ranches and farms. National groups such as the American Farmland Trust, Trust for Public Land, The Nature Conservancy, and the Rocky Mountain Elk Foundation also strongly support easements.

Who is opposed?
A few western stockgrower associations remain unconvinced. Their dedication to protecting ranchers' rights is worthy of respect. However, conservation easements are a very American expression of a landowner's right to use their property as they see fit. The tool is just another option for ranchers to consider. It will work for some and not for others. Ranchers who have done easements are the best source of real-world information. Ask them.

What kind of land can be protected by a conservation easement?
The IRS criteria for tax-deductible easements reveal that many kinds of land are eligible. Ranches most often qualify because they contain significant open space, agricultural land, ecological values, and historic resources. However, the baseline report is the proper way to determine the specific criteria under which the land may qualify.

Who can donate an easement and who can receive one?
Any owner of land that contains significant conservation resources may donate a conservation easement. If a mortgage exists, the lender must subordinate its interest to prevent the extinguishing of the easement should a foreclosure occur. If tax deductions are claimed, the easement donation must be made in perpetuity to a qualified 501(c)(3) nonprofit conservation organization or unit of government.

Is an easement forever?
If tax deductions are claimed, it must be forever. Term easements exist for a set period of years, but most land trusts accept only perpetual donations.

What kinds of restrictions are typical? Isn't every easement the same?
Each conservation easement is different. However, prohibitions on surface mining, timber clear-cutting, transferring all water rights, waste dumps, feedlots, and other destructive practices are the norm. Ranching activities are supported. Land subdivision and development are heavily restricted, but partial developments are possible if carefully designed. Some land trusts seek projects with no additional houses. Others assist landowners in meeting their financial needs through lot sales while conserving the majority of a ranch.

Do I have to allow public access?
No. You control public access the same as before.

What about mineral rights?
If you own the mineral rights, you must prohibit hard rock, placer, and other forms of surface mining. Oil and gas development may occur unless it would destroy significant conservation values. Such development is typically allowed if it is in line with state laws about density and reclamation.

If you don't own your mineral rights, a professional geologist must assess the ranch and write a letter saying the likelihood of "commercial mineral development is so remote as to be negligible." Then the easement can be donated and tax benefits received. If commercial mineral potential exists, this disqualifies the property for tax incentives. However, such cases are extremely rare.

What about water rights?
Most easements require that the water rights necessary for continued agricultural operations and ecological function stay with the property. Transfer of surplus water rights might be allowed in special cases, but most land trusts prefer to keep all water on a property.

Will the easement interfere with ranch management?

Won't the land trust become a nuisance in day-to-day ranch management?

If you donate your easement to a group you know and trust, such nuisances will not occur. Easement holders have a responsibility to visit the property at least once a year to assure that houses have not been built where you promised they wouldn't be built. Ranch conservation easements essentially leave grazing, fencing, irrigation, and weed and predator control up to the landowner.

If you are being asked to give up a land use right you need, seek another group that matches your philosophy. If, after careful consideration, the deal still won't work, don't donate a conservation easement. Walk away.

Am I locked into my current agricultural practices?

No. Easements are written to allow for future innovations that do not damage the ranch's significant conservation values. While restrictions on plowing certain lands may be part of the easement, you retain your flexibility to adopt new agricultural practices.

What happens if the land trust decides I have committed a "violation" of the conservation easement?

Of the 7,500 easements in the United States, only twelve violations have had to be resolved in court. In all these cases, a house or other structure was either built or proposed where it was not allowed. The courts have consistently ruled in support of easements. If the landowners broke their word and built a structure, it had to be moved or demolished. The Land Trust Alliance did a recent study and found that smaller "violations" of easements occur but are resolved through conversations, not lawsuits. A rancher should keep the easement simple with very clear statements of what can and cannot be done on the land. Never sign a conservation easement you are uncomfortable with or work with a group you are unsure of.

What happens if the land trust I work with goes out of business?
A backup holder of the easement can be identified in the document. You can even stipulate who will *never* hold the easement—including specific groups or the government. If no specific backup holder is named, a court chooses a suitable receiver.

Can a third party environmental group start enforcing the easement?
No. Conservation easements can be written with a clear prohibition against such intrusions. This prevents "third party beneficiaries" from being involved with your easement.

Won't a conservation easement prevent me from borrowing money?
No. Loans are made based on the remaining agricultural and other value of a ranch. Lenders routinely make operating and other loans on ranches under easement. If a ranch is still worth $1 million after the easement, a loan request for $50,000 is a no-brainer for a lender. Some donors have said the easement kept their borrowing in line with agricultural needs and prevented the creation of excessive debt.

What if my heirs need to sell the ranch?
They can sell the ranch anytime for whatever price the market will bring. The easement is likely to reduce the market price of a ranch but does not "freeze" it. Over the years, appreciation will restore a portion of the land's value that was donated away. In fact, some buyers are willing to pay substantial amounts for a conserved ranch with scenic and wildlife amenities. In cases where partial development is allowed under the terms of the conservation easement, the income received may reduce the need to sell the ranch.

What if my ranch is surrounded by subdivisions and the value of my place is very high?
In such cases, a conservation easement may not be the best choice. You may wish to sell that ranch and buy a place farther out for less money and invest the remainder. You may also find a "conservation buyer" who wants the ranch mostly for open space purposes.

Will the conservation easement reduce my property taxes?
Probably not. In most cases the easement land is already in an agricultural assessment class. Property taxes might go down in states where such taxes are based on potential use rather than current use.

How much will it cost to donate a conservation easement?
It may cost between $10,000 and $20,000 to complete an easement if tax deductions are being claimed. The income and estate tax benefits of the easement gift usually amount to many times that amount.

Legal and accounting fees vary depending on the complexity of the deal but are generally not excessive. The land trust can draft the easement deed into a standard format for the landowner's lawyer to review. This can save the landowner money in legal fees, but the land trust's boilerplate easement will be written from the land trust's point of view and the landowner will probably want to negotiate some changes. The baseline report can cost $3,000 or more but may be done by the land trust if the donor cannot afford it. A land appraisal can cost $5,000 or more. The Stewardship Endowment contribution is typically $5,000–$10,000 but is negotiable. Hiring a land planner is necessary only if you are interested in developing part of your property. Sieve mapping and a conservation land plan can cost $5,000 or more.

Aren't easements just like zoning and other land use planning regulations?
No. Easements are voluntary and may provide financial compensation. Government regulations such as zoning are based on "police power" authority, are not voluntary, and provide no money for their restriction of development rights. Regulations change under political and economic pressure. Conservation easements are forever.

How do conservation easements compare with deed restrictions and restrictive covenants?
Deed restrictions can prohibit land subdivision just as a conservation easement can. However, enforcement is up to the individual who restricted the land prior to sale. For this reason, deed restrictions are seldom enforced because of legal costs. They tend to perish with the individual who originally sold the land. No tax benefits come from deed restrictions since any kind of property can be restricted and no "qualified conservation" organization is involved.

Restrictive covenants are commonly used to control house sizes and colors, nuisances, outside lighting, and other design issues. Covenants are enforced by a homeowner's association made up of lot owners and can be changed or eliminated by a vote of the members. This device is only as strong as people want it to be.

In contrast, conservation easements are a legal interest in land whose restrictions are enforced by an incorporated group with a fiduciary responsibility to do so. If the land trust fails to monitor and enforce an easement, the attorney general of the state and the U.S. Treasury Department could attempt to revoke their tax-exempt status. A land trust will go out of business if it does not enforce the easements it holds.

What is a Purchase of Development Rights (PDR)?
A PDR is a purchased conservation easement. It is far less common than donated easements because land trusts have a hard time raising the money. Some states have programs funded by sales taxes, gambling proceeds, and general revenues. The Federal Farmland Protection

Program has limited funding but is highly competitive and requires a minimum 25 percent contribution by the land trust.

Isn't it wrong to decide how a ranch will be used forever? What about future needs?
We decide the fate of land every day when subdivision plats are filed at the county courthouse. Residential development is a *permanent* conversion of land. A conservation easement leaves many land use options open, including the possibility of legally extinguishing the easement if its conservation purposes can no longer be fulfilled.

Doesn't common law prohibit ruling from the grave on how land is used?
Conservation easements avoid the "rule against perpetuities" in two ways: the land trust is legally "immortal," and the easement can be voided in the future if its conservation purpose can no longer be fulfilled through no fault of the landowner. In such cases, the landowner and land trust meet with a judge who rules that the easement is extinguished and the development rights are merged with the underlying ownership. Such cases have yet to occur, but may in future years as development surrounds easement properties.

Why should I donate a conservation easement when groups I don't respect use the same tool?
Any tool can be used in ways we support or oppose. A conservation easement is a private real estate transaction used by people of all philosophies to achieve their goals. It is not an assault on our freedom.

Do city or county governments have the power to prohibit conservation easements and their federal tax benefits?
No. If we believe in private property rights, we must acknowledge the right of any landowner to place a conservation easement on his or her land. Otherwise, we are empowering local

governments to regulate the private real estate marketplace. That is antithetical to free enterprise.

Aren't conservation easements an assault on private property rights?
Absolutely not. They are a true expression of private property rights. Landowners—not government agencies or zoning officials—are deciding the future of their ranches. Conservation easements are a way of exercising our constitutional right to own and use land as we see fit. Those who oppose this tool are free to do so but not on the grounds that conservation easements reduce liberty.

Won't the easement force me to be a tenant on my own land?
Not any more than transferring water rights or mineral rights would. You are the titleholder to the property; the easement is a "non-possessory interest"—it is not physical ownership of the land.

Won't the federal government take away my land if I give an easement?
This is one of the most curious rumors about conservation easements in the West. We know of no case where this has occurred. Although the federal government can condemn property for roads or power lines whether a conservation easement exists or not, it must pay fair market compensation for the land taken. This price is often in dispute. However, we searched in vain for the name of one individual who donated a conservation easement only to have the federal government somehow confiscate their land. This is a rural legend, not a fact.

What about all the negative things I hear about conservation easements?
Get the facts.
Talk to ranchers, agricultural organizations, and land trusts that have completed conserva-

tion easements. There are a few self-appointed "experts" out there who earn their living spreading misinformation and paranoia. Ask them if they have any real-world experience with the technique. Chances are they don't. Ask them for the names of the "officials, bankers, and landowners" in their horror stories about conservation easements. Odds are they will come up empty.

Conservation easements are not for everyone, but the device is extremely sound and proven in the American marketplace.

Looking southeast to Tres Montosas Mountain, Montosa Ranch.

3 Assembling Professional Advisers

The best way to regain control of your destiny as a rancher is to be clear about your goals and understand all your options. Then you can make informed decisions about the long-term future of your ranch. This is a daunting task. But unless it's done, you and your family risk making a poorly informed, costly choice.

Knowledgeable professional advisers can provide you and your family with help in evaluating your options. Typically, you will need the following advisers:

- attorney
- financial adviser
- appraiser
- conservation land planner
- land trust
- real estate developer—for conservation developments
- real estate broker—for conservation developments

Find people you can trust to be on your team. One of the greatest threats to keeping a ranch in the family is the estate tax. For this reason, it is important to find advisers who specialize in estate planning. If you are interested in combining conservation of your ranch with estate planning, then find advisers who are experienced in conservation easements. Discuss what you want to achieve with other ranchers and people in your area who understand your situation, but also be prepared to think outside the local box. To make sure that the advice you are receiving includes the latest estate planning–land conservation options, it may be helpful to look at what is happening in other parts of the country. Of all the western states, Colorado and Montana are probably furthest ahead on the learning curve. The Colorado Cattleman's Agricultural Land Trust, the Montana Land Reliance, the Taos Land Trust, and the Sonoran Institute in Arizona are examples of good resources. There are also national land trust organizations such as the Land Trust Alliance, the American Farmland Trust, the Trust for Public Land, and The Nature Conservancy that can bring a broader perspective to your situation.

Estate planning does not happen overnight. Neither does designing and implementing a conservation easement on your land. Both will require time and money. But it is an investment in your business and your land. Keep in mind that neglecting a plan could cost your family more than creating one.

Attorney and Financial Adviser

Because of the serious legal and financial consequences involved with estate planning, your legal and financial advisers are critical. Sometimes the same individual fills both roles. He or she should have experience in all the related tax and legal matters in connection with your estate.

Conservation easements are a legal specialty that requires in-depth knowledge of the relevant tax laws. Make sure your attorney has this expertise. If this expertise is not available in your area, it may be possible for the local attorney or financial adviser with whom you feel comfortable to affiliate with an outside attorney who is experienced in this field.

A model conservation easement is often a good place to start (see the Appendix). Keep in mind that every conservation easement is different and customized to fit the specific needs of each landowner. Some landowners will make an outright gift of the development rights on their property. This is the simplest conservation easement to draft. Other landowners may reserve certain rights, including the right to develop a limited number of housesites. These are more complicated transactions.

A good way to keep your legal costs down is to be as clear as possible about your goals. Then ask your lawyer how many times he or she has helped other clients accomplish similar outcomes. It will also help if you know the right questions to ask. This book will help you in this regard.

Appraiser

Under the tax laws you must hire an appraiser to perform a qualified appraisal anytime you make a charitable contribution of property with a claimed value over $5,000. Otherwise, the gift may be disallowed as a tax deduction. The value of a good appraisal can't be overemphasized. This is because, in an audit with the IRS, the qualifications of the appraiser and the thoroughness of their research will be scrutinized.

Appraising a conservation easement is complicated. Finding an appraiser with the necessary experience can be challenging, especially in states that lag behind in the use of conservation easements. As with attorneys and financial planners, it may be possible for the local appraiser with whom you feel comfortable and who knows the local real estate market to affiliate with an outside appraiser who is experienced with conservation easements. When looking for a competent, qualified appraiser, make sure they are licensed and certified by the state. In addition, professional appraiser accreditation programs such as the Accredited Rural Appraiser (ARA) designation can help you make sure the appraiser is qualified.

Two guidelines govern all appraisals, including those on conservation easements.

One is the "Yellow Book," the *Uniform Appraisal Standards for Federal Land Acquisitions*. You can get a copy of this from the federal government. The other is the *Uniform Standards of Professional Appraisal Practice* (USPAP). All appraisals must comply with these minimum appraisal standards. Another helpful resource is *Appraising Easements* published by the Land Trust Alliance.

Finding "comparable sales" is a challenge in states where conservation easements have not been widely used. If this is the case, make sure the appraiser includes conservation easement properties as part of the research for the appraisal—either from in-state or from out of state. A land trust can help you identify such properties.

At best, an appraisal is a well-informed estimate of the value of your property, one that depends on the vagaries of the real estate market to provide comparable sales of similar land.

To make sure you are not surprised by the appraisal, it is a good idea to meet with the appraiser *after* they complete gathering data but *before* they commit anything to writing. Find out what the appraiser anticipates the written report will say. Some landowners ask for a preliminary appraisal to determine whether to proceed with an easement transaction. If the numbers appear to be acceptable from a financial standpoint, the final appraisal report is then prepared. For landowners who are philosophically committed to the easement, the appraisal number is a secondary factor in their decision making.

Conservation Land Planner

A land planner is necessary in two cases:

- If you want to hire a consultant to complete the baseline report and represent you in negotiations with the land trust.
- If you want to develop part of your ranch in order to realize your financial and estate-planning goals.

A conservation land planner brings a different mind-set to the table than a conventional planner who is primarily concerned with short-term economic expedience. The goal of conservation land planning is to create the long-term appreciation of land value. This is accomplished by preserving the integrity and beauty of the natural environment. In addition, a conservation land planner should be sensitive to (1) your concerns as a rancher, (2) environmental and ecological concerns, and (3) the requirements of the tax laws related to conservation easements.

The conservation land planner also brings to your team a graphic capability that is valuable as a marketing tool in illustrating the quality of the land analysis with good maps. These maps provide an inventory of your property to determine what land is to be protected and where it is appropriate to build. This graphic inventory factors in ecological, ranching, archaeological, and open space concerns. In short, the land planner provides you with a visual representation of your options. Do you place the entire ranch under a conservation easement (in which case further land planning may not be necessary)? Or, do you reserve a limited number of house sites for possible future development? If the latter is the case, how many house sites are possible or desirable? Where are they located? How do you keep them from conflicting with your ranch activities? The graphics are useful as an analytical tool and for quickly communicating and evaluating the overall concept of the project.

In addition, the graphic materials also provide the real estate broker with a story to sell, one based on a land plan rooted in the landscape. The story reveals the way the development has been designed to protect the most valuable natural resources both for the continued operation of the ranch and for the quality of life in the development. The graphic materials help demonstrate the added aesthetic and land value the conservation easement provides the prospective buyer.

Land Trust

If you want to combine conservation of your ranch with estate planning, it is important to identify a qualified conservation organization such as a land trust to help you. A land trust can be a valuable source of information and guidance as you examine your options.

The land trust (or other qualified group) receives the conservation easement. Most land trusts are private, nonprofit corporations presided over by a board of directors consisting of volunteers from the community in which the land trust operates. A government entity can also be the receiver. In order for the donation of a conservation easement to qualify for federal tax benefits, the land trust must be a qualified conservation organization with 501(c)(3) status.

This group must monitor and enforce the development restrictions contained in the conservation easement. Monitoring responsibilities include inspecting the property each year to verify that no violations of the conservation easement have occurred. Enforcement responsibilities include hiring the lawyers necessary to enforce the terms of the conservation easement should serious violations exist that cannot be resolved through discussions with the landowner.

The land trust becomes your partner in the long-term management of your land.

It provides the institutional longevity that allows you to control how your land is managed when you and your immediate family are no longer living or the land has been sold.

The Colorado Cattlemen's Agricultural Land Trust (CCALT) operates as part of the Colorado Cattlemen's Association and has a mission to "help ranchers and farmers protect their agricultural lands and encourage continuing agricultural production." Stockgrowers' groups in Nevada, Wyoming, California, and other states have formed similar trusts.

CCALT has now completed some eighty conservation easements on 152,000 acres of ranchland. Their director, Lynne Sherrod, and the majority of the board are all ranchers. Lynne speaks plainly about the group: "It is a land trust OF landowners, BY landowners, and FOR landowners." They focus on clear, effective conservation easements that "protect ranches and facilitate their intergenerational transfer to heirs that want to work on the land." In Colorado and the entire American West, conservation easements have been widely accepted because they are voluntary and may provide financial compensation.

When selecting a land trust it is important to find the right match between your interests as a rancher and those of the land trust. Organizations such as the Land Trust Alliance and the Trust for Public Land can help provide you with contact information for groups in your area, and may be able to direct you to a logical choice. The Land Trust Alliance maintains a database of land trusts by state with contact information (see lta.org). There are many land trusts to choose from. Discuss your particular situation with several and answer the following questions:

- Are the goals and values of the land trust consistent with your own? Determine if the land trust is sensitive to the needs and challenges of ranching. Meet with the board of directors. Ask to examine the land trust's written criteria for accepting a conservation easement.
- Is the land trust stable? Review the history of the organization and its land conservation record. How long has it been in existence? Does it have a paid executive director and staff? Ask about its financial status, including its stewardship endowment fund. It is in your interest for the land trust to be not only solvent but also financially healthy so it can perform its responsibilities for monitoring and enforcing the development restrictions contained in the conservation easement.
- Can the land trust provide you with technical assistance? Some trusts can complete most of the needed documents for the easement transaction. Others prefer to have land conservation planning consultants do this work.

Real Estate Developer

If your goal is to get some of your money out of the ranch by subdividing and selling lots, you should consider hiring a real estate developer as part of your team. The developer can help you with the subdivision approval process. This varies by county, but often includes surveying and platting the property, preparing the Disclosure Statement, the Water Quantity and Availability

Plan, the Water Quality Plan, the Liquid Waste Disposal Plan, the Solid Waste Management Plan, and the Terrain Management Plan. The developer is also responsible for processing all applications, plans, maps, and other entitlements related to the project as well as obtaining the approvals and permits required by all applicable government agencies. The developer can also help you to market the property by hiring and paying a real estate broker. Make sure that your agreement with the developer stipulates all of the developer's responsibilities, including the provision of liability insurance.

Typically, the developer is paid a commission based on lot sales. The idea is to make sure the developer is on the same side of the financial table with you. However, there may still be a conflict of financial interests. For example, as the landowner, you may be interested in allowing the creation of only a limited number of carefully sited lots designed to protect the rest of the ranch. The developer may be interested in selling as many lots as possible—regardless of what happens to the ranch. For this reason it is critical to make sure the developer supports your concept for the project. Find someone who philosophically agrees with what you are trying to do. Even though the developer may not share the same emotional attachment to the land you have, they should be able to understand the real value that is created by a well-designed conservation easement. The goal of the design should be to sell the last lot for more than you sell the first lot.

The following question may help a developer grasp the conservation development concept: What would a prospective buyer be willing to pay more for—a lot surrounded by protected land or a lot surrounded by unprotected land with unknown future development possibilities?

If the developer still can't understand land protection as the value-adding principle in the development of your land, then find someone else.

Another criterion for selecting a developer is access to the growing marketplace of conservation buyers. Conservation buyers will shy away from someone with a bad record in land protection. Find out the reputation of the developer. Integrity is everything.

Real Estate Broker

The real estate broker is responsible for showing the property to prospective buyers and closing sales. The broker should be licensed and in good standing with the state realtors association. Check on the broker's reputation with other brokers as well as with former clients. The broker should be familiar with the market for ranch real estate as well as with the market for recreational properties. They should be capable of marketing the property through both local and national networks, and be skilled at promoting the property on the Internet and through publications, direct mailings, and other marketing devices.

Like the developer, it is important for the broker to "buy into" land protection as the value-adding principle of your development. One of the great marketing advantages of conservation development is that it provides an excellent product to sell, one with integrity based on an ecological land use plan. Conservation easement design creates value by allowing the buyer to feel good about doing good: the opportunity to be part of a larger conservation effort to leave a legacy of land stewardship to future generations. Preserving the beauty of the land is something meaningful that people are increasingly buying into.

You Decide

When selecting advisers, trust your instincts. If someone comes highly recommended, but you sense that he or she is full of hot air, find another adviser.

Looking west to the foothills of the Mimbres Mountains, Lake Valley Ranch.

4. The Baseline Report

The design of an effective conservation easement depends on a competent analysis of the subject property. Writing restrictions without a sound understanding of the land is unprofessional and may leave significant conservation values unprotected. This damages the credibility of easements and threatens the long-term existence of the federal tax deductions. Landscape analysis is an essential starting point in easement design.

Project Scoping

How much landscape analysis is enough? Every conservation easement requires a solid baseline report. Cases with a substantial development component may need sieve mapping, which uses overlays of soil, slope, wildlife habitat, plant communities, historic resources, visibility, and other factors to properly locate homesites away from significant conservation resources (see Chapter 6). Project scoping determines the amount of investigation needed.

The following levels of landscape analysis are recommended:

- Standard Baseline Report—for conservation easements with a few family-member building envelopes or homesites.
- Basic Sieve Mapping and Baseline Report—for conservation easements with moderate development within or adjacent to the protected land.
- Detailed Sieve Mapping and Baseline Report—for projects where the conservation easement is part of a major development.

The Baseline Report

The baseline report is used to qualify the property for tax benefits, identify significant conservation values for protection, establish the condition of the property at the time of the easement donation, and serve as a basis for long-term stewardship. It is created based on fieldwork, research, and interviews with the landowner and other experts. In some states the baseline report is filed as Appendix A of the conservation easement deed to serve as part of the official record of the project. However, the conservation easement deed is the instrument of record for resolving all violations.

The baseline report is not an all-inclusive inventory of the natural environment. It contains a thorough but concisely written assessment of vegetation, wildlife, landforms and soils, water, historic resources, and improvements. The point of the baseline report is to identify the property's significant conservation values clearly so they can be protected, not to generate a complete natural history or reams of statistical data.

Preparing the baseline document requires diverse skills and the ability to see interrelationships in the landscape. It also requires organization and the ability to listen. Research for the baseline report starts with an interview of the landowner. The landowner will often be a primary source of information on the natural environment, history, management, and countless other things about the ranch. The baseline report is both a compilation of facts and the results of a shared experience of learning the land.

Besides the landowner interview, three critical steps begin the baseline process:

1. Geologist's Assessment. If the mineral rights are not owned by the rancher, a geologist must evaluate the mineral potential and determine if it is "so remote as to be negligible" (see Chapter 2).
2. State Historic Preservation Office (SHPO) Search. The legal description of the proper-

ty is sent in for a search of the SHPO's records for sites and structures that are on or are eligible for the National Register of Historic Places. General archaeological resources or the trace of an historic trail are typically found. Sometimes a structure is found that warrants being listed on the Register if the landowner wishes.
3. Natural Heritage Program Search. The legal description is also sent to the Heritage Program to determine if threatened or endangered species are found on the property. Their brief report will indicate the closest locations of rare species. This is not cause for alarm. The presence of an important plant or animal means that ranch management is compatible with the continued survival of that species.

The preceding three steps should be taken as soon as possible because the necessary letters and reports may take several weeks or months to receive.

Fieldwork is done following archival research, reviews of land management plans, interviews with agency personnel, and the preparation of an accurate base map. Competent professionals usually take no longer than one or two days to assess a property in the field regardless of size. The key is to include all the necessary information without getting lost in the details. Precise measurements of natural features are usually not needed. Mapping their location and describing their characteristics are sufficient. Except in special cases, detailed statistical analyses should be avoided because they become overly time-consuming during annual monitoring. However, all major improvements such as buildings must be carefully documented.

Fieldwork is typically done using a base map, aerial photo, camera, and notebook. Consultants and land trust personnel now often use a Global Positioning System (GPS) to locate structures, building envelopes, and other key features precisely.

Beyond the technicalities, a quality baseline report depends on the skills and perceptions of the preparer. Baselines are unlike other natural resource inventories. The goal is to understand the landscape as a whole. Complex natural features should be concisely described and mapped with an eye on how the conservation restrictions can be written to protect significant conservation values.

Once the fieldwork and research have been completed, the baseline report is prepared.

Formats vary widely from simple to complex. There is no standard format. However, an effective baseline should contain the following documents:

- Dated Cover Page—Identifies the landowner and the preparer of the baseline report. (1 page)
- Table of Contents. (1 page)
- Owner Acknowledgment Statement—Includes a brief summary of the land's acreage, location, and present condition. A signature line must be included for the Grantor (landowner) and Grantee (land trust). (1 page)
- Summary Information—Includes landowner information, zoning, directions, conservation values, supporting government polices, a statement of how the property qualifies as a tax-deductible conservation easement, and a summary of conservation easement restrictions and reserved rights such as building envelopes. This section also includes a map showing the property boundaries and topography. Some baselines also contain a regional map indicating the location of the subject property. (2 pages and 1 map)
- Introduction—Includes a history of the conservation project, a statement of the baseline report's purpose, a summary of the conservation values to be protected, and the extent of investigation. (1 page)
- Land Uses and Management—Includes a description of the historic and current land uses on the property. This description gives a context for continuing uses such as ranching. Adjacent management practices on federal and state land are also described to show how the easement supports public values. (1 page)
- Structures and Improvements—Includes a list of all structures, major ranch roads, irri-

gation ditches, fences, gravel pits, water rights, wells and windmills, mineral rights, rights-of-way and easements, grazing leases, and neighboring properties with contact information. All structures and gravel pits must be shown on a map to be included in this section. Roads should be mapped if they are restricted or when development is part of the easement design. It is not necessary to map fences, wells, windmills, and other routine ranch features because they will generally not be restricted. Land trusts often want a copy of all water rights documents for their files, but this is not included in the baseline. (2 pages and 1 map)

- Conservation Values—Includes maps and descriptions of the conservation values. This is the core of the baseline report. (6 pages and 2 maps)
- Physical Description—Describes the ranch's physiographic province (e.g., the Basin and Range), the ranch's eco-region (e.g., the Chihuahuan Desert), and the area climate. (1 page)
- Geology and Landforms—Describes bedrock geology, glacial history, landform types and related soils (from the Natural Resources Conservation Service survey), and the existence of minerals (drawn from geologist's report). General landform types, such as alluvial valley bottom, canyon, outwash terrace, granite mountain, and limestone mesa, are shown on a map to be included in this section. Natural hazards such as debris flows, fault lines, and earthquakes are briefly evaluated. (1 page and 1 map)
- Hydrology—Highlights all rivers, creeks, wetlands, and groundwater features. If a major waterway exists, its annual hydrograph, flow regimes, and Federal Emergency Management Area "floodplains" are discussed. The floodplain can be shown on the General Landform map as a separate landform type to distinguish it from other portions of a valley. Hazardous material sites, if any, are located and described. (1 page)
- Vegetation—Describes and maps basic vegetation types. Typical descriptions are "sagebrush grassland," "ponderosa pine forest," "Gambel oak woodland," "riparian mosaic,"

and "Sonoran Desert scrub." Federal Forest and Range Habitat Types are often used. The location, patterns, and condition of vegetation types are discussed and the most common trees, shrubs, forbs, herbs, and grasses are mentioned with both common and Latin names used. Range condition is usually described as excellent, good, fair, or poor rather than quantified by transects or "stubble heights." Grazing can be addressed in a Ranch Management Plan, but most ranch easements do not require one. Rather, the rancher's self-interest and ability are relied upon to manage his or her own place. If a rare species exists, its populations are located and information is provided on its abundance, condition, and ecology. Weeds, forest management, fenced paddocks, and other matters are also discussed. In most cases ranch management will not be changed. (1 page and 1 map)

- Wildlife—Describes species that use the property, including big game, predators, raptors, migratory birds, fish, and reptiles. Wildlife agency personnel and the rancher are often the best sources of information for these data. If bird counts exist, they are included in an Appendix of the baseline. If a rare species exists, it may be necessary to prohibit tree cutting (e.g., around a bald eagle nest) or to make a similar accommodation. Usually, little change of ranch management is needed. (1 page)
- Historic Values—Describes the results of the SHPO search. If the resources are highly sensitive, the exact information is not given in the baseline report to avoid their destruction by trespassers. If a structure is determined to be on the National Register, then it should be protected by the conservation easement. Information about the general history of the ranch is given as a rationale for protecting the ranch. This includes a history of the settlement, ranching, mining, and subdivision in the area. (1 page)
- Open Space Values—Explains the visibility of the site from scenic byways, wilderness areas, national monuments, or other public lands. A property can also qualify if it offers sweeping vistas of a ranching landscape. Nonscenic lands such as watersheds,

buffer zones, and other sites also qualify. Government planning and open space policies also help with qualification. (1 page)

- Appendix A: Photographs and Photo Points Map—This is an *essential* part of a baseline report. Numbered photographs are included that illustrate all structures and representative examples of ecosystems and their condition. The photographs are cross-referenced by number to a map that shows the exact photo point of each photograph. Ten to twenty pictures are typical to adequately describe the conditions on a ranch. Photos (3″ x 5″) are mounted two on a page along with a descriptive caption and compass bearing for each photograph. These photographs are the primary way to document the baseline conditions of a ranch and to identify easement violations. They should be taken every year during the monitoring visit to create a permanent record of the ranch's condition over time. Also included in the baseline report should be a statement such as "due to the dynamic nature of vegetation communities, these photographs should be used mostly to confirm violations of restrictions on the construction of buildings, mining, signs, and other prohibited improvements; shifts in plant community proportions are considered natural." However, clear-cutting of timber and habitual overgrazing a ranch are not exempt if these changes are prohibited in the conservation easement. (7 pages and 1 map)
- Appendix B: Geologist's Mineral Report—Printed on the geologist's professional letterhead, this report outlines the bedrock of the site and the existence of any commercial minerals. The "Remoteness Test" is met if the geologist concludes that "the likelihood of commercial minerals is so remote as to be negligible." (2 pages)
- Appendix C: Species Lists—This may include a Bird Count List, Mammals List, a Plant Species List, biological assessments, public land management status for adjacent lands, and other relevant materials related to the ranch's qualifications. The Heritage Program's letter on Threatened and Endangered Species and the State Historic

Preservation Office report should be included in Appendix C if and only if their findings do not compromise the location of the resource described. For example, if a bald eagle nest or a major archaeological site exists, indicate that the evidence is on file with the easement receiver and the government agency, but do not identify that location. Never file a baseline report that would aid a poacher or pothunter. (1 page)
- Appendix D: References—Includes all sources, including interviews with experts. (1 page)
- Appendix E: Qualifications and Contact Information for Report Preparer. (1 page)

A typical baseline report runs about thirty pages including five maps. Some land trusts use shorter formats; others require more detail. There is no single best style. As long as the report qualifies the property for tax deductions, describes its present condition (in text, maps, and photographs), and allows for clear monitoring, the document is sufficient.

The baseline report can also be a bridge between the "Old West" and the "New West"—a way of transmitting hard-won knowledge of land and life to future generations of landowners. Ranchers are often the best source of information on the history of their place. Conservation easements are simply a written contract to use the land wisely over the long-term. In the end, stewardship is an ethical value that is far more durable than any legal agreement. Words do not conserve land; people do.

Looking south to Magdalena Mountains, Tres Montosas Mountain, and San Mateo Mountains, Montosa Ranch.

Ancient Native American settlement, looking east to Magdalena Mountains, Montosa Ranch.

The conservation easement design process serves a triangle of interests: the landowner's, the land trust's, and the land's. The goal is not utopia but a privately owned landscape with every chance of remaining beautiful, productive, and environmentally sound. The most destructive practices are prohibited. For the rest, we must trust the stewardship of ranchers with support from land trusts.

Crafting an easement is based on negotiation. The landowner and the land trust each will have certain bottom-line requirements. The protection of significant resources described in the baseline report is the common ground. Typically, the land trust has a boilerplate easement, which can be used as a starting point and amended. Sometimes the landowner's attorney drafts the easement. Negotiations determine if the landowner and land trust share a common vision. If so, the deal may be completed. If not, the landowner seeks another receiver. Finding a good match of philosophies is essential.

The Conservation Easement Deed

A conservation easement is a permanent commitment. *Its restrictions are perpetual.* Although the document can be amended, this is not assured and takes time. Easements can be extinguished in highly unusual circumstances, but this should not be expected. The crafting of easement restrictions requires focus, forethought, and sound professional advice. See Chapter 3 for advice on assembling professional advisers, and the Appendix for an example of a Model Conservation Easement Deed.

A conservation easement deed contains three basic parts:

- "WHEREAS" statements. These outline, in clear language, the reasons for creating the easement (to conserve ranchland, open space, wildlife habitat, and other conservation values). They also confirm that the local comprehensive plan, government policies, and federal and state easement laws support the creation of the easement, and that the land contains significant conservation resources. These clauses make the basic case for the easement gift. They are critical for a "plain language" legal interpretation of the easement in future decades.
- Consistent uses. This is a listing of what *can* happen on the land. Land uses that support sustainable ranching are allowed.
- Inconsistent uses. This is a listing of what *cannot* happen. Land uses that damage significant conservation resources are restricted or prohibited.

The remainder of the deed recites legalities related to monitoring, enforcement, perpetual duration, transfer of the easement to a named receiver, amendment, and other matters (see Appendix). An attorney should carefully review all sections. Rather than focus on these technicalities, we will discuss the core of an easement—the restrictions on land use.

Easement restrictions must be unambiguous and enforceable. Vague wording only leads to confusion and unintentional violations. The best easement language clearly identifies what can and cannot be done on a property. However, most deeds contain limitations on certain land uses rather than outright prohibitions.

All future land uses can be addressed in a conservation easement deed. The following limitations are commonly addressed.

Subdivision
What part of the ranch will be placed under a conservation easement? All of it? If not, what parts are either excluded or allowed to be subdivided to provide income? How many homesites will be held back for family members or for sale? Specifically, where will they be, or can

they be located later? Does the landowner want to retain the right to subdivide and sell part of the ranch to another rancher for agricultural purposes? All scenarios must be considered, and the numbers run to better understand the financial implications of each scenario. If you choose to prohibit the subdivision of your land for nonagricultural (meaning residential) purposes, the following restriction is included:

> Division, subdivision, or de facto subdivision of the Property, whether by physical or legal processes, for nonagricultural purposes is prohibited.

For projects where lots or building envelopes will be created, the conservation easement deed must say that this is allowed and must identify the locations report. The deed must also contain a clause that grants all remaining development rights to the land trust for extinguishment.

Buildings and Other Structures

Ranch structures such as barns, sheds, fences, wells, windmills, corrals, and stock pens are usually not restricted except to exclude them from particularly sensitive sites. These structures can be built, enlarged (to a specified maximum square footage), repaired, or replaced without any prior notice to the land trust. Residential dwellings are restricted in number and location, with similar allowances made for repair and replacement. Some easements restrict both building height and color, and prohibit reflective roof materials. Others avoid these design matters.

Mining

If you own the mineral rights, *you must prohibit all future surface mining*. Otherwise, the donation of the conservation easement will not qualify for a federal tax deduction. The use of gravel from existing pits for on-ranch purposes is allowed within a specified number of acres. Any commercial use of gravel is prohibited. If a rancher wants a large commercial gravel pit, that

Room blocks, ancient Native American settlement, Montosa Ranch.

area is best excluded from the easement. Oil and gas wells may be permitted if those rights are owned by another party, and if they don't destroy the conservation values of the property. If the landowner owns the oil and gas rights, the land trust may want to prohibit development or negotiate a limit on the density and location of wells.

Water

It makes little sense to "conserve" a ranch if the water rights can be severed from the property. Therefore, most land trusts will ask you to prohibit the transfer, lease, or sale of water rights belonging to the ranch. Some groups will accept a partial or temporary transfer of "wet water" as long as the water rights are not transferred and sufficient water remains for historic levels of agriculture and for creeks and wetlands. Easements often prohibit or limit the alteration of natural stream channels. For example, a natural stream or river may not be dammed and riprap may not be placed on its banks. Small check dams to control erosion and stock tanks are typically allowed. Maintenance of irrigation ditches, and the creation of new ditches is allowed because irrigation is essential to maintain many ranches.

Roads

Additional roads are restricted by stating if and where they can be built and what kind of surface material is allowed. The right to create new dirt roads for agricultural purposes is retained by the rancher. The maintenance and repair of existing roads are also allowed.

Grazing

Livestock management is left up to the rancher.

A maximum number of animal units (AUMs) is sometimes stipulated. Some ranchers use vegetation condition information to keep a future owner from overgrazing their land; others are opposed to this practice. Each case must be negotiated on its own merits. The baseline information describes a mutual understanding of the condition of the land at the time the conservation easement is donated. The goal is a plain sense interpretation of the land that includes natural cycles of drought and changes in rangeland health. However, the land trust may ask you to prohibit or limit grazing in riparian areas. If that's a deal breaker, find another group to work with. If you agree to any limitation on riparian grazing, a violation would result from systematic use, not from cows knocking down a fence once in a while. The violation of a grazing restriction has never led to court enforcement of a conservation easement.

Timber Harvest

Each land trust will have a different policy regarding forest management. Clear-cutting is typically prohibited in easements. Most trusts seek to limit logging to a specified amount per year for noncommercial, on-ranch purpose or to deal with insect infestation, disease, and fuels reduction. Other groups support thinning and selective logging to improve habitat. Thinning of communities such as piñon-juniper woodlands are often allowed to reverse the effects of encroachment and restore ecosystem health. Timber management is sometimes addressed in a separate Forest Management Plan prepared by a competent forester.

Industrial/Commercial Uses

In-home businesses can continue at the ranch headquarters; other commercial activities must be negotiated. Feedlots, waste dumps, manufacturing, landfills, and other major commercial uses are typically prohibited. Each land use, particularly feedlots, must be carefully defined to avoid unintentionally banning a needed activity. The processing and sale of agricultural products originating on the ranch are often allowed.

Recreation

De minimis (minimal) recreation uses such as hunting, fishing, hiking, and horseback riding present no problem. The use of off-road vehicles and snowmobiles for nonagricultural purposes is often prohibited to protect significant resources. Most land trusts will want to prohibit golf courses, ski areas, and other intensive developments. In some cases a golf course area can qualify for an income tax deduction but would not qualify for the additional estate tax benefits found in the Taxpayer Relief Act of 1997 (see Chapter 8). Conservation easements that allow lot owners to have recreational access to the conserved part of the ranch can be designed if they avoid harming significant conservation values.

Predator Control

All lawful control measures are allowed.

Herbicides and Pesticides

The use of legal biocides is allowed. Aerial applications are often prohibited because of wind drift problems but may be negotiated on a case-by-case basis.

Public Access

Access is completely controlled by the landowner. The overwhelming majority of easements grant no rights to the public to enter the property.

Sometimes a separate recreation management agreement that grants public access under very strict conditions is written outside of the easement. This can benefit ranchers along river corridors, in hunting areas, or wherever trespassing has become so common that it is best dealt with by allowing regulated public use. "Walk-In Hunting Areas" are an example. State fish and game agencies will often enforce this access agreement and deal with poaching, harassment of livestock, litter, noise, parking, and other matters. Such agreements should be signed for a specified period. One-year agreements are best until the landowner gains confidence that the access is being managed properly. After that, ranchers often sign five- or ten-year agreements.

Trash Dumping

The storage, dumping, or other disposal of toxic materials or noncompostable refuse is prohibited. The storage of agricultural chemicals is allowed. Metal parts, old barbed wire, and other ranch materials are permitted at a specific site.

Miscellaneous Land Uses

Restrictions on cell phone towers, satellite dishes, utilities, pipelines, airstrips, billboards, signs, docks, and species introduction are negotiated. Game farms are typically prohibited.

Restrictive Covenants

Some landowners wish to address house sizes and colors, outside lighting, road maintenance, pets, noise, and other matters associated with building envelopes and lots. Many land trusts do not want the problems associated with monitoring and enforcing such restrictions. Restrictive covenants are an appropriate alternative. They are written prior to lot sales and enforced by a Homeowner's Association. It is important for the ranch owner to be a voting member of the Homeowner's Association, preferably with veto power. The Homeowner's Association can change the covenants through a vote of the members. This is a potential weakness. If it is essential to protect something, put it in the conservation easement deed. If it is less important, address it with covenants and hope the lot owners comply.

Every conservation easement deed is different. It is best to stay focused on the basic restrictions covering rights to subdivide, develop, mine, harvest timber, and engage in commercial/industrial uses. Since conservation easements are voluntary, land trusts that hold out for highly stringent restrictions risk having landowners walk away.

Conservation easements that are designed simply to protect the land or allow a few family member homesites are fairly straightforward. Easements that allow a limited subdivision are more complex and require more detailed restrictions. In all cases, protecting the property's significant conservation values is the key. The aim is to keep the place in production as a working ranch.

Looking southeast to Tres Montosas Mountain, Montosa Ranch.

Sieve mapping is a six-step design process that allows the landowner to protect the conservation values of the land while creating a limited development to raise some money. The objective is to protect the integrity of the land, prevent unplanned development, and promote the appreciation of land values over time.

The Definition

Sieve mapping is a design process that promotes a *qualitative* analysis of the land to help determine where conservation is most important and development can be best placed to protect the intrinsic qualities of the land that enhance the long-term value of the ranch—in other words, where to build and where not to build.

In contrast, the *quantitative* analysis of conventional development focuses on the number of lots and on the other factors of development that influence the short-term conversion of land value into cash.

Two facts raise a critical question. First, developers are not rewarded by the appreciation of long-term value; they are rewarded only by the profit margin at the time of the initial sale. Second, the enhancement value of open space contributes positively to the individual property owner's equity. The critical question is this: How can the short-term profit that motivates the individual developer be harnessed to the creation of long-term property value?

Sieve mapping suggests an answer. It is a way of capturing the conservation value of the land for the short term as well as the long term. As an alternative to the conventional pattern of land development typified by Sangre de Cristo Ranches (see Chapter 1), sieve mapping is based on preserving the integrity of the natural landscape as a value-adding principle of development. The criterion for success is the enhancement of land value in the short term, and the appreciation of land value in the long term.

The History

Sieve mapping is rooted in a tradition that views human beings as part of nature, not separate from it. This tradition found a worthy advocate in Frederick Law Olmsted Jr., an early twentieth century American landscape architect. In 1919 Mr. Olmsted observed that "a local park adds more to the value of the remaining land in the residential area which it serves than the value of the land withdrawn to create it." This is because buyers prefer lots that are adjacent to or are near parks. Olmsted's insight about the enhancement value of parks, when translated onto the rural landscape, is the basis of sieve mapping. Using it, we can identify and then capitalize on the economic value of land conservation in the marketplace.

Sieve mapping was refined in the 1960s by Ian McHarg in his widely acclaimed book *Design with Nature*, and more recently by Randall G. Arendt in *Conservation Design for Subdivisions*. McHarg asks, "Can we not create from a beautiful natural landscape, an environment inhabited by man in which natural beauty is retained?" Sieve mapping helps provide an answer to this question as well.

Several studies of the enhancement value of open space help ground the idea in economic reality. A 1967 analysis of a ten-acre neighborhood park in Lubbock, Texas, found that "within a two-and-one-half block area around the park, land values declined with distance from the park." This relationship was true for the sales price of land only—not houses and land—a fact with revealing implications for land developers. A 1978 study in Boulder, Colorado, found that "the existence of greenbelts had a significant impact on adjacent residential property values." The relationship proved to be linear: a $4.20 decrease in the price of residential property for each foot away from the greenbelt. The aggregate property value in one of the neighborhoods studied was approximately $5.4 million greater than it would have been without the greenbelt.

These studies quantify the economics of open space conservation. They demonstrate that, as Mr. Olmsted observed, open space *does* affect the surrounding land market in positive ways. Unfortunately, the reverse is also true. Poor planning can cancel the enhancement value of open space. Witness the example of *Forbes'* "Sangre de Cristo Ranches" in southern Colorado or the "Wild Horse Ranch" in southwestern New Mexico. The result of this poor planning is diminishing land values. In contrast, when thoughtfully integrated into a ranch, a limited development not only contributes to the intangible value of making a place more enjoyable for living, it also improves the economic bottom line.

The Process

Step 1: Identify the Conservation Areas

The first step is to decide where you should NOT develop. This is accomplished by systematically identifying the conservation areas to be protected. Reviewing the baseline report is a good starting point, if one has been completed. It makes good sense to protect those areas that most enhance the long-term value of the remaining land to be developed. However, this depends on subjective judgment. What intrinsic qualities of the land are most valuable to a rancher? to a developer? to a homeowner? to an ecologist? These different value systems may result in conflict and compromise. But the beauty of sieve mapping is that it allows these different viewpoints to be reflected in the final design. Each can be mapped on the land as a way of finding common ground and avoiding conflict. Most important, the sieve mapping design process lets the existing features of the land determine where and where not to build. It is a value-based process that is rooted in the landscape, not imposed on it.

Walking the land several times to gain a thorough personal familiarity with the place best accomplishes the first step. This firsthand experience helps the designer to really get to know the land and discover its meaning. The maps and their contours stop being mere abstractions. This firsthand experience can be supplemented by listening to the insights of the rancher who has lived on the land through all four seasons. When does that arroyo flow? When do the winds come and from what direction? What are the most significant qualities of the landscape in terms of topography, climate, drainage patterns, wildlife habitat, agricultural lands, cultural sites, views into the site from existing public roads, and views from the site toward features such as distant mountain ranges? All of these important features are identified in the field using aerial photographs or Global Positioning System (GPS) techniques.

Step 2: Map the Information
The second step is to create overlay maps. Each overlay corresponds to a separate value of the landscape to be protected. For example, Figure 6.1 maps "Nonbuildable Peaks." These are areas on top of ridgelines and peaks (down 40 feet below the tops) that should be protected from development. This restriction is based on the idea that it is preferable to have the horizon defined by a natural ridgeline rather than by a human-made structure, and that keeping the natural horizon free from such structures will enhance the value of the property.

Figure 6.2 maps "Water Bodies and Drainage" as special places in the arid landscape of the American West that should be off-limits to development. Figure 6.3 maps "Wildlife Habitat" (roughly corresponding to "Water Bodies and Drainage") as a priority for conservation. Protecting these areas makes common sense from both an ecological point of view and a marketing point of view. Protecting wildlife habitat or ridgelines, for example, is a conservation value that also protects the buyer's investment in the land.

Figure 6.4 maps "Prime Agricultural Land" as an intrinsic value to be protected. This value is based on more than range or crop production. Agricultural land contributes significantly to

6.1

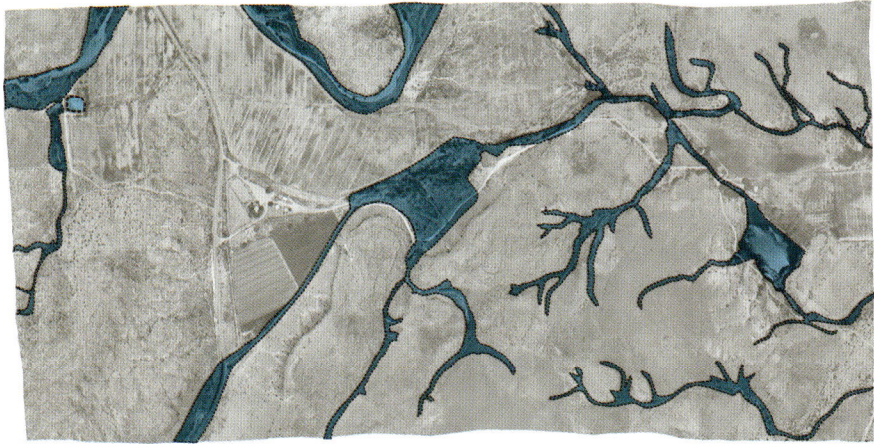

6.2

Figure 6.1 | Nonbuildable Peaks: To protect the natural horizon from human-made structures, this overlay maps the hills and ridges down to 40-contour-feet below the tops of the hill or ridge as being off-limits to development.

Figure 6.2 | Water Bodies and Drainage: This overlay corresponds to land located within 150 feet on either side of a water body or natural drainage system. This land is being protected from development in order to preserve the natural drainage pattern of the land.

Sieve Mapping 73

Figure 6.3 | Wildlife Habitat: This overlay corresponds to wildlife habitat (roughly corresponding to water bodies and drainage). This land is being protected from development in order to preserve the natural habitat of wildlife.

Figure 6.4 | Prime Agricultural Land: This overlay corresponds to prime agricultural land that is being protected from development in order to preserve agricultural productivity.

6.3

6.4

the scenic beauty so many people are looking for. Lot buyers value open space and are willing to pay for it. Protecting prime agricultural land is another win-win.

Figure 6.5 maps "Historic and Archaeological Sites" as contributing to the intrinsic value of the land. Figure 6.6 maps "Steep Slopes" not because of the positive value derived from protecting them, but rather because of the negative consequences of developing them. The erosion caused by building on steep slopes diminishes land value and costs money to repair.

Figure 6.7 maps the "Public Viewshed" corresponding to that part of the property that is visible from the public highway. By protecting this viewshed, the experience of driving through the rural landscape is preserved for the benefit of both the homeowners and the public. Preserving this viewshed helps to qualify the property for the tax benefits that can result from donating a conservation easement.

Step 3: Synthesize the Information

The third step is to create a composite of all the overlays (see Figure 6.8). This reveals an overall pattern of conservation priorities. It is an organic pattern based on the intrinsic qualities of the land and on what is perceived to be important to protect. The land that falls through the "sieve" of conservation priorities is the land that is more appropriate for development. *It is also the land whose market value is most enhanced by the protection of what is not developed.* The gray area on the composite map of conservation areas becomes the red area on the map of buildable land (see Figure 6.9).

Step 4: Designate the House Sites

Figure 6.10 illustrates "House Sites Relative to Buildable Land." Designating the house sites within areas that are appropriate for development is best accomplished by walking the land and field-verifying the information. Optimal sites are located based on views to the surrounding

Figure 6.5 | **Historic and Archaeological Sites:** This overlay corresponds to historic and archaelogic sites. This land is being protected from development in order to preserve the cultural heritage left by previous inhabitants.

Figure 6.6 | **Steep Slopes:** This overlay corresponds to the land where the slope exceeds 25 percent. This land is being protected from development to prevent damage due to erosion caused by building on steep slopes.

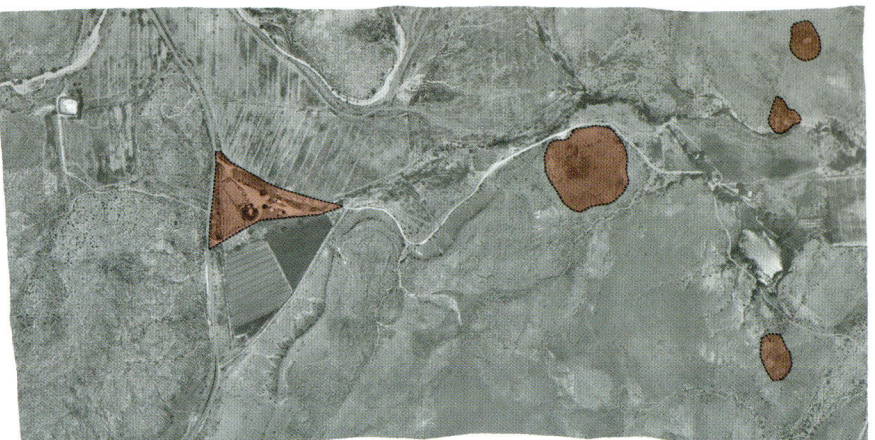

6.5

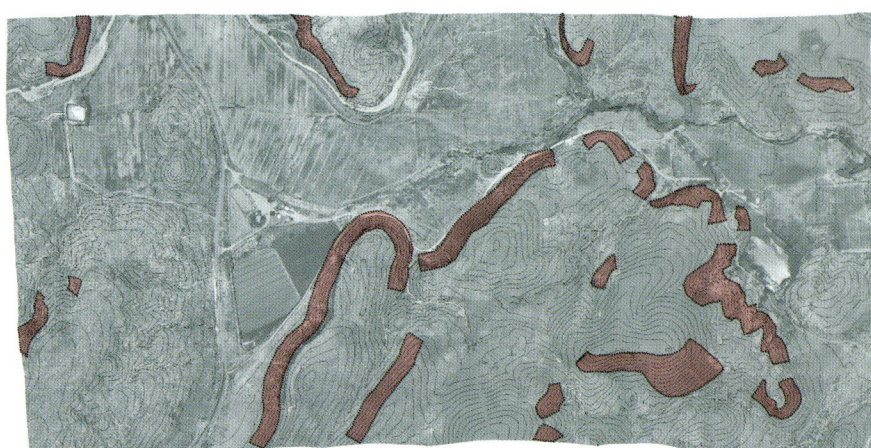

6.6

landscape, visibility of other homes, landscape relationships (topography, vegetation, water), and the cycle of seasons (wind, sun, precipitation). Photographs are taken to document the relationship of each site to the landscape and an analytical diagram is created (see Figure 6.11). These diagrams have the potential to serve as a tool for (1) better understanding the land, (2) proving the appropriateness of the homesite, (3) graphically marketing the development, and (4) helping ensure that the individual house sites complement the site-sensitive quality of the overall design.

Step 5: Lay Out the Roads
The following principles guide the laying out of roads:

1. Avoid crossing areas prioritized for conservation.
2. Make the roads as inconspicuous as possible by following contours and avoiding long, straight sections.
3. Minimize the length and cost of new roads.
4. Where possible, use existing roads.

Designing roads based on these conservation principles may add to the initial cost, but these expenses are offset by the enhanced value of the house sites. This contrasts with the road design criteria used in conventional development that is primarily quantitative: minimize costs by keeping roads short, straight, and avoiding steep slopes.

Figure 6.7 | Public Viewshed: The public viewshed is identified as that part of the study area that is visible from the public roadway. To protect this area, it is mapped as being off-limits to development. By protecting the viewshed, the experience of driving through the rural landscape leading up to the house sites is preserved for both the homeowners and the public.

Figure 6.8 | **Conservation Areas:** This is a composite of the preceding maps shown in Figures 6.1–6.7. It reveals a pattern of conservation priorities—an organic pattern based on what is perceived to be important for protection. The land that falls through the "sieve" of conservation priorities is the land that is appropriate for development. It is also the land whose value is most enhanced by the protection of what is not developed. The gray area on this composite map of the conservation areas becomes the red area on the following map of buildable land (Fig. 6.9).

Figure 6.9 | **Buildable Land:** The red area on this map corresponds to the gray area of the preceding map of conservation areas (Fig. 6.8). It is the land that has fallen through the "sieve" of conservation priorities.

opposite

Figure 6.10 | **House Sites Relative to Buildable Land:** Designating the house sites within the areas identified as being appropriate for development is best accomplished by walking the land and field-verifying the optimal sites based on views to the surrounding landscape, views to the other house sites, and the relationship of each site to the landscape (topography, vegetation, water) and the cycle of the seasons (wind, sun, precipitation).

Figure 6.11 | **Analysis of House Site:** To prove the appropriateness of each house site, photographs are taken to document the relationship of the site to the landscape. In addition, an analytical diagram of each site relative to the features of the landscape is created.

6.8

6.9

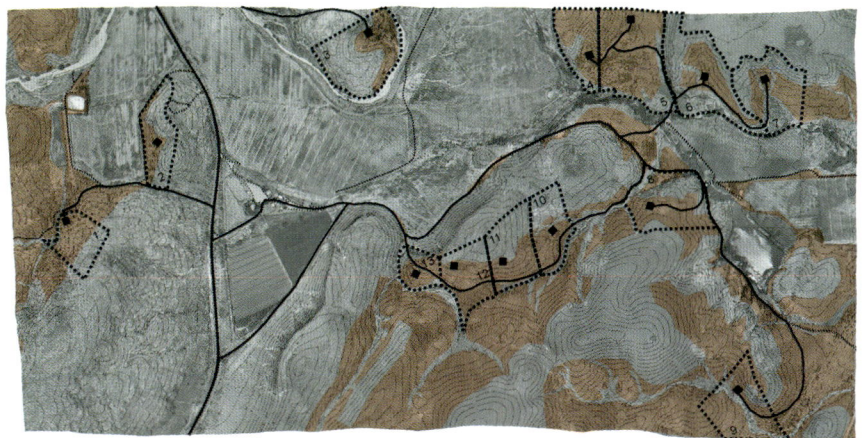

6.10

6.11

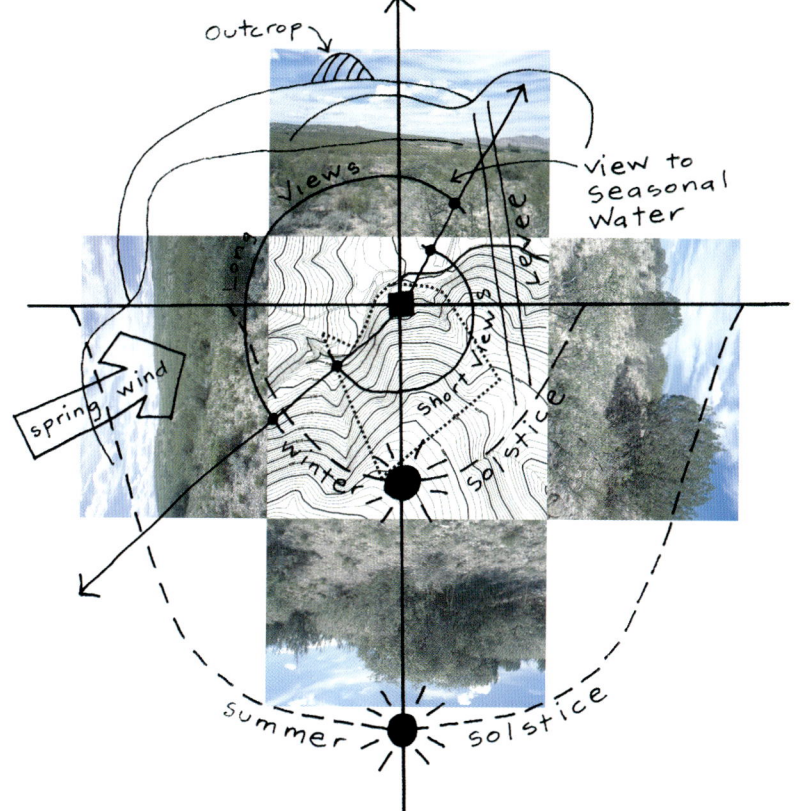

Sieve Mapping 79

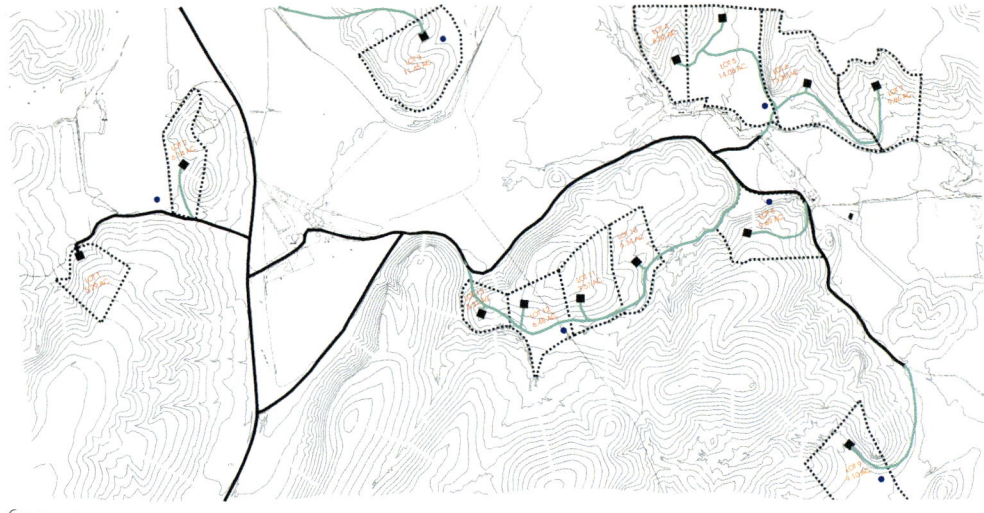

6.12

Figure 6.12 | **Conservation Development:** Once the conservation areas have been identified, the house sites designated, and the road alignments determined, drawing the lot lines is a mere formality. However, there are at least two possible legal frameworks for accomplishing this formality. One is to subdivide all the land into plats of fee simple ownership. The other is to create an open space development with smaller platted areas of fee simple property with the owners sharing an undivided interest in the remaining open space. In either case, houses can be built only on the designated house sites. The remaining land—whether individually or jointly owned—is protected from development by a conservation easement. This figure depicts an open space development.

Step 6: Draw the Lot Lines

Once the conservation areas have been identified, the house sites designated, and the road alignments determined, drawing the lot lines is relatively straightforward. However, there are at least two ways to accomplish this. One is to subdivide all the land into plats of fee simple ownership. This is typically what happens in a conventional development. The other is to create an open space development with smaller platted areas of fee simple property with the owners sharing an undivided interest in the remaining open space that continues to be grazed by cattle. In either case, houses can be built only within designated building envelopes. The remaining land—whether individually or jointly owned—is protected from development through a conservation easement.

The Comparison

Now let's look at conservation development versus conventional development. Figure 6.12 illustrates a conservation or "open space" development based on the sieve mapping design process. This pattern offers several advantages. By allowing only the smaller lots to be fenced, the remaining areas are left completely open for shared uses such as horseback riding. The smaller lot sizes also minimize the maintenance responsibilities for the individual owner. The main advantage to the buyer is that of a "virtual ranch": the pleasure of owning part of a responsibly managed working cattle ranch without having to take personal care of it.

Figure 6.13 contrasts a conservation development with a conventional development where all the land is subdivided into lots. It is important to note that even though the lot sizes are smaller in the conservation development, the number of lots remains the same. Keeping the number of lots constant allows the comparison to emphasize the qualitative advantages of the conservation development and its impact on lot prices. What would the buyer be willing to pay more for—a lot surrounded by protected land or a lot surrounded by private land with unknown future development possibilities?

Sieve mapping works as a design process because it improves the effectiveness of land conservation and because buyers prefer land that is adjacent to protected open space. This is the basis for identifying and then capitalizing on the economic value of land conservation in the marketplace. Sieve mapping is a way of asking the land to reveal discrete conservation qualities that, when superimposed, reveal patterns of conservation priorities coinciding with economic expedience. These priorities are not arbitrary because they are based on the land. The functional objective is a productive working landscape. They are also based on the value system of the landowning rancher. Those areas that are cherished by the rancher can be so identified and protected. And the economics are not just expedient. They are based on the long-term creation of real property value premised on land protection as a principle of development that appreciates over time.

Figure 6.13 | **Conventional Development:** It is important to note that although the lot sizes are smaller in the conservation development compared with the lot sizes in this conventional development, the number of lots remains the same. For purposes of comparison, the density of the development is neutral. Keeping the number of lots constant allows the comparison to emphasize the qualitative advantages of the conservation development and its impact on lot prices. What would the buyer be willing to pay more for—a lot surrounded by protected land, or a lot surrounded by unprotected land with unknown future development possibilities?

Sieve Mapping 81

Willow at edge of human-made lake, Lake Valley Ranch.

Conservation Development

Conservation development is based on land protection as a value-adding principle. The value is added in two ways: through site-sensitive design and planning that identifies and protects the conservation values of the ranch, and through the use of a conservation easement that prohibits future development of the land in perpetuity. Buyers can be sure that the protected land will never be developed. This certainty creates economic value.

This approach works for ranchers who need to develop part of their ranch, but who want to minimize the impact the development will have on their land. Ranchers may choose to develop to get part of a lifetime's worth of investment out of the land for retirement or estate planning purposes. Some may want to create an income opportunity that allows them to take advantage of the income tax benefits that result from donating a conservation easement. (Donating a conservation easement provides an income tax advantage only when there is income to shelter; it provides an estate tax benefit whenever there is equity in the land. See Chapter 8.) Whatever the reason, conservation development seeks a win-win solution: a win for the rancher in achieving financial and conservation goals, and a win for the land in minimizing the impact of development.

Advantages of Conservation Development Based on Sieve Mapping

1. Conservation development creates long-term value by preserving the integrity, stability, and beauty of the land by minimizing the visual and environmental impacts of new development on critical resources. Conventional development destroys long-term

value by ignoring the visual and economic impacts of new development on the very resources that make the land attractive for development in the first place.

2. Conservation development creates value by preserving open space. Conventional development destroys value by subdividing all the land for private use. Buyers prefer lots that are adjacent to or are surrounded by protected land to lots that are adjacent to or are surrounded by private land with unknown future development possibilities.
3. Conservation development creates value by giving the buyers more for their money. It demonstrates how you can buy a smaller lot and enjoy the entire ranch's open land designated as off-limits to development. Compare this with buying a conventional 40-acre lot and having the use of only that 40 acres.
4. Conservation development creates value by allowing the land-rich and cash-poor rancher to take advantage of conservation easements. Such easements provide income tax benefits only when there is income to shelter.
5. Conservation development creates value by allowing the buyer to feel good about doing good: being a part of a larger conservation effort to leave a legacy of land stewardship to future generations. The buyer is buying a lot while helping to "save the landscapes of the American West." Preserving the integrity of the land is something meaningful that people can buy into.

Conservation development works *only* when the conservation easement restrictions meet the tax law requirements that the gift be made "for conservation purposes"—ecological, open space, recreational, and historic values. This is why it is essential to begin a conservation development project by identifying the conservation values of a property that must be protected.

The crux of conservation development is balancing land development with land protection. This balance has to do with not only *where* development is appropriate, but also *how much* development is reasonable. Figure 7.1 illustrates the factors that influence this balance. Sieve mapping is a rational design process for determining where and where not to develop, but only the landowning rancher can decide how much development achieves his or her goals. This depends on immediate financial needs as well as on a sense of responsibility for succeeding generations. For many ranchers this decision boils down to the following question: Can we promise our children the inheritance of a physical environment at least as good as we have inherited?

Conservation development offers a compromise for the landowning rancher and for the buyer. The compromise for the rancher is twofold. First, any development will impact the land; the objective is to minimize the impact. Second, a conservation development that consists of a limited number of appropriately located lots may or may not result in less income for the rancher than if the entire ranch is developed. But the rancher preserves the ranch and the conservation values of the property that make the place worth keeping. The rancher also gets the personal reward of conserving the land. The compromise for the buyer is paying more money for less land. But the buyer gets the certainty of knowing that the surrounding landscape that is protected will never be developed. The buyer also gets the personal satisfaction of participating in conservation.

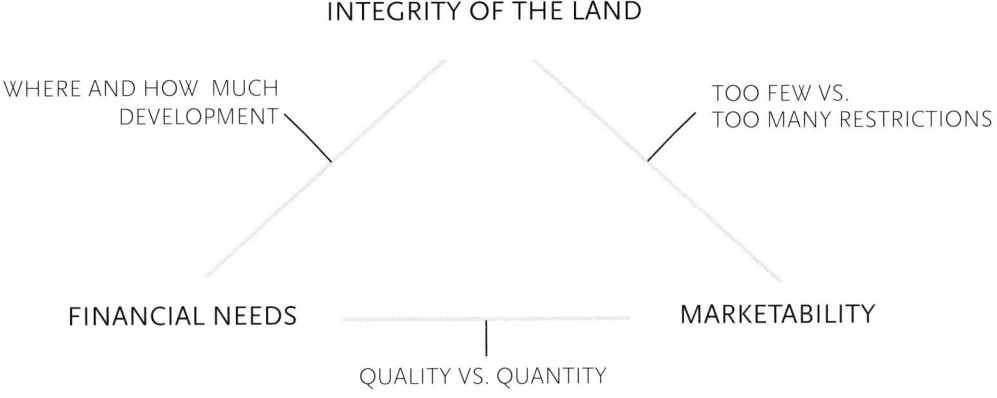

Figure 7.1 | Conservation Development Balance

Drafting Conservation Easements to Avoid Conflict

Whenever residential development is introduced into a working agricultural landscape, there is inherent conflict. A conservation easement can be an important tool in mediating this conflict. How the conservation easement restrictions are written is critical. Avoid legalese. Write the restrictions in plain English. The easier it is for the landowner to understand the restrictions, the easier it will be for the land trust to monitor and enforce the restrictions.

Conservation Development Design 85

Make sure the "purposes clause" is clearly written to define what you are trying to protect. This is especially important for successor generations of landowners who are not party to the drafting of the conservation easement. A court of law will look at the plain language of the easement. If the language is not plain, the court will try to divine the intent of the parties who wrote the conservation easement based on a "reasonable person" criterion. You do not want to open the door for the court to interpret the easement.

Avoid terms of art such as "best management practices," "historic agricultural use," or "sustainable yield." If you have to use such terms, define and quantify them. For example, when restricting future subdivision of the land, clearly define what you mean by "subdivision" so that it is not subject to interpretation. (For example, does a subdivision involve lots of more than 35 acres when state law may exempt 35-acre lots from subdivision laws?)

When restrictions border on subjectivity, include a "performance clause" to help clarify them. For example: "The purpose of restricting the height of buildings is to preserve the pristine view from adjacent lots."

Another idea for mediating conflict is to incorporate management plans as part of a conservation easement. This allows the easement to grow and live as a document. For example: "Agricultural uses of the property shall use stewardship and management practices generally consistent with the standards of the Natural Resources Conservation Service or other commonly acceptable sound management. Such management can include any innovative agricultural practices that produce improved economic viability of the ranch, and do not cause any reduction in the present range condition."

Avoid standard goals and arbitrary restrictions. For example: "The land has a carrying capacity of X cow/calf units." Such arbitrary restrictions are meaningless because they do not take into account the vagaries of rainfall. As any responsible rancher knows, a ranch's carrying capacity varies with precipitation.

Be sure to draft the easement with an eye on the restrictions and rights that you, as landowner, want to retain and on the restrictions and rights you are willing to give up. Do you want to retain the grazing rights on the lots to be sold? Are the lot buyers allowed to hunt on the entire ranch, or are they limited to their lot only? Keep in mind that a buyer probably will not be willing to purchase a lot without acquiring significant control over what happens on the lot.

Conservation Easements and Restrictive Covenants

The best way to define the future of a property is to draft the conservation easement and the restrictive covenants at the same time. This will flush out any issues that might be of concern. You don't have to reinvent the wheel. Start with a model conservation easement and a model declaration of restrictive covenants. The restrictive covenants, also known as the Covenants, Conditions, and Restrictions (CC&Rs), are enforced by the Homeowner's Association and are not the responsibility of the land trust. These models will help you focus on issues that you might not have otherwise thought about. Then customize each document to reflect any additional concerns and preferences you may have. It will also be helpful to draft the Homeowner's Association bylaws to better understand how any unanticipated control issues can be resolved in the future. Succession of ranch ownership and ongoing ranch management are big issues that need to be worked out *before* any lots are put on the market.

What goes in the easement and what goes in the covenants? It depends on the parties involved. The restrictions that protect fundamental conservation values should go into the easement. The more stringent restrictions (such as those governing the construction materials and colors of the houses) are more difficult for the land trust to enforce and should be kept out of the easement and put in the covenants.

When drafting the restrictions that go into the easement, it is helpful to keep in mind the difference between the landowner's interest and the land trust's interest. For the landowner, one of the advantages of a conservation easement is that the land trust assumes the responsibility for enforcing the restrictions, including hiring the lawyers to do so. Because of this responsibility, it is in the land trust's interest for the restrictions to be unambiguous and clearly enforceable. The more complex the restrictions become, the more difficult and expensive the conservation easement is to monitor and enforce. The land trust does not want to get bogged down with ambiguous or subjective restrictions. It must evaluate the proposed restrictions in terms of its ability to monitor and enforce them. As the landowner you don't want it to be any other way. You should shy away from a land trust that does not take this stewardship responsibility seriously.

An example of how the interests between the landowner and the land trust can differ has to do with monitoring and enforcing the restrictions governing the house sites. It is in the landowner's interest for these restrictions to be included as part of the conservation easement. This is because including them in the conservation easement—as opposed to the restrictive covenants—will make the restrictions final. The buyers of the lots will be less tempted to try to negotiate a revision to the restrictions. If the restrictions are in the restrictive covenants, the sophisticated buyer will know that before a Homeowner's Association is formed to enforce them, the restrictive covenants are controlled by the seller and therefore can be changed for the sake of a sale. Including the restrictions in the conservation easement deed helps define exactly what is being sold. However, it may not be in the land trust's interest to assume the responsibility of enforcing these restrictions. Restrictions governing the location of building envelopes are unambiguous (they can be defined by a survey), and are clearly enforceable. Similarly, restrictions governing the allowable floor area and height of houses are also unambiguous and clearly enforceable. In contrast, restrictions governing construction materials and colors are subject to time-consuming interpretation and, from the land trust's point of view, may be too risky.

In the process of drafting the conservation easement, the landowner and the land trust negotiate the restrictions to be included in the conservation easement. These negotiations are based on evaluating the financial risks associated with enforcing the restrictions compared with the financial resources in the stewardship endowment fund that are available to cover the risk. Since the landowner is typically required to make a financial contribution to the stewardship endowment fund, the negotiations involve offsetting the monitoring and enforcement responsibilities with an increase in the stewardship endowment contribution. It may also be possible to provide the land trust with a special supplementary assessment right to cover cost overruns that may result from special restrictions that are important to the landowner.

From a legal perspective it is helpful to think of segregating restrictions into a hierarchy:

1. Deed of Ranch Ownership is the title to the land.
2. Conservation Easement Deed is the perpetual donation of some or all development rights, monitored and enforced by the easement receiver.
3. Restrictive Covenants are the day-to-day restrictions in the development, enforced by a Homeowner's Association.
4. Deed of Lot Ownership is the title that goes to the lot buyer.

The most "senior" deed is the title to the land held by the rancher. Next is the Conservation Easement Deed. The most fundamental restrictions for protecting the land are in this deed. Because the Restrictive Covenants are recorded after the Conservation Easement, they are "junior" to the Conservation Easement Deed. The restrictions for protecting the development are in the covenants. If the Conservation Easement Deed is for protecting the conservation values of the land, the Declaration of Restrictive Covenants is for protecting the real estate values of the development. The Deed of Lot Ownership, recorded last, is for protecting the property rights of the lot buyer.

What is being marketed in conservation development is not so much real estate as a package of protected amenities. From a marketing point of view the intent of the restrictions must be to add value. There is an optimal balance between too many restrictions and too few. Excessive control can drive away buyers, lower demand, and subtract value. Too little control can take away from the quality of the overall development and reduce the value of lots. Figure 7.1 illustrates a triangle of considerations that must be balanced in a successful conservation development.

Unless a buyer perceives that the protected open space is legally assured *in perpetuity*, prices will not hold up. For this reason it is essential that the entire land plan be completed and the conservation easement be finalized before the lots are marketed. Protecting the integrity of the lots is as important as protecting the integrity of the surrounding open space. This is especially true when the size of the lots is large enough for significant future subdivision.

How do you prevent further subdivision of these lots?

One possibility is to sell the lot with the understanding that the buyer would place a conservation easement on the land once it is purchased. An advantage of this approach is that it may help the buyer to justify a higher purchase price because of the subsequent income tax benefits from placing a conservation easement on the property. The disadvantage of this approach is that it depends on trust between seller and buyer. *There can be no formal legal agreement without negating the potential tax benefits to the buyer.* The conservation easement must be *voluntarily* donated to obtain the tax benefits; the Internal Revenue Service will disallow a quid pro quo. As a result, this approach leaves the rancher selling the lot exposed to the possibility that the buyer would back out on his or her promise to place a conservation easement on the land after it is purchased.

Another possibility is to sell the lots with a conservation easement already placed on them. The advantage of this approach is that it removes the uncertainty of relying on trust between the seller and buyer. The disadvantage is that the potential tax benefit to the buyer for placing the lot under a conservation easement cannot be used to justify a higher purchase price. The tax benefit derived from donating a conservation easement goes entirely to the seller, who may or may not be able to take full advantage of it.

Timing

The donation of a conservation easement is applied against income earned in the year of the gift. The date of the gift is the date the conservation easement is recorded. Only 30 percent of adjusted gross income may be deducted in any one year. The unused deductible amount can be carried forward for the following five years. Because of this "carryforward" rule, the optimum time to record a conservation easement deed is when the first lot is sold (so that there will be more income against which to take the tax deduction). This can be accomplished by placing the conservation easement deed in escrow, with instructions to the escrow officer to record it immediately prior to the sale of the first lot.

Another timing factor to consider in conservation development has to do with the "shelf life" of the appraisal. Section 1.170A-13(c) of the federal Treasury Regulations states that the appraisal must be done not earlier than 60 days before the date of the easement contribution (the date the easement is recorded), and not later than the due date (including extensions) for the property owner's income tax returns. For example, if the easement is donated in December, the appraisal would have to be completed between the October preceding the donation and the following 15 August (assuming an extension of time to file the return is requested). One way to evaluate the potential tax benefits of a conservation easement donation before making the donation is to conduct a preliminary appraisal. The cost of a preliminary appraisal is about 75 percent of the cost of a full appraisal because much of the same research and analysis must be completed. Another way is to conduct a complete appraisal with the expectation of having it updated at the time of the easement contribution.

Thinking It Through

There is no single best way for completing a conservation development. Giving away certain development rights in order to protect most of the ranch in perpetuity while simultaneously adding value to the land that is set aside for limited development can be complicated. Further, "in perpetuity" is a difficult concept to grasp. As someone once said, "Forever is a long time—especially toward the end." No one wants to be cursed by his or her great-grandchildren for decisions made today.

Here are some questions along with a suggested sequence of benchmarks to help determine if conservation development is right for your situation:

1. What are your financial goals?
2. If your heirs inherited your estate today, how would the estate tax bill be paid?
3. If you were to sell a limited number of lots, what are the restrictions and rights that you, as landowner, want to retain, and what restrictions and rights are you willing to give up?
4. Seek a land trust or other receiver to discuss a possible easement donation.
5. Find a conservation easement attorney; get his or her advice.
6. Have a title report prepared for the property.
7. Hire a conservation land planner; complete the Baseline Report and Sieve Mapping.
8. Begin conservation development design; line up a developer and real estate broker.
9. Locate an appraiser.
10. Draft the Conservation Easement, the Declaration of Restrictive Covenants, and the Bylaws of the Homeowner's Association.
11. Complete preliminary appraisal.
12. Comply with any county or state subdivision requirements, including drafting any required "disclosure statements" that must be consistent with the conservation easement and restrictive covenants.
13. Survey and submit the preliminary plat of the subdivision for county planning review.
14. Negotiate the final Conservation Easement, including the Stewardship Endowment Fund, with the land trust.

15. Finalize the Declaration of Restrictive Covenants, and the Bylaws of the Homeowner's Association.
16. Approval of final subdivision plat by Planning Board and County Commission.
17. Record the approved plat.
18. Complete the appraisal.
19. Place the signed conservation easement in escrow with instructions to escrow officer to record the easement immediately BEFORE the sale of the first lot.
20. Begin real estate marketing.
21. Complete lot sales.
22. Stewardship. Rancher continues to manage conserved areas. Land trust does annual monitoring of the land under conservation easement. Homeowner's Association enforces restrictive covenants in force on the lots.

Patience

Completing a successful conservation development may seem like a real chore, and certainly the complexity of this process should not be underestimated. But with the help of competent advisers, patience, and a personal commitment to a solid outcome, ranchers can achieve something that can be and has been of great help to them all across the West.

Cattle grazing in Sacaton grass, Lake Valley Ranch.

Human-made lake, Lake Valley Ranch.

Ocotillo, Lake Valley Ranch.

The following are important questions to consider in financial and tax planning:

What would the combined federal and state estate tax be on your estate?
How will your heirs pay those taxes?
Who will inherit your ranch and who will run it?
What is the greatest threat to maintaining your ranch in agricultural production?

How you and your family's legal and financial advisers answer these questions will help you clarify your goals.

The financial advantages of conservation design and development come from two principle sources:

- Private property rights and how they are valued
- Federal and state income and estate tax incentives for conservation easement donations

Valuation of Property Rights and Conservation Easements

Property rights in the United States are based on the concept of fee simple title. This means that a landowner is vested with all the rights necessary to treat land as a fully marketable commodity. Fee simple ownership of the land consists of many different property rights, such as the right to graze livestock, the right to harvest timber, the right to sell water or minerals, the right to subdivide, and the right to build houses. Any of these rights can be separated and legally conveyed in the marketplace. Subsurface mineral rights, for example, are commonly bought and sold separately from surface rights.

How real estate is appraised depends on the value of these different property rights. For example, land can be valued based on its capacity to produce a commodity such as cattle. Or land can be valued based on its capacity to produce nontraditional commodities such as scenic views, wildlife habitat, or open space. How land is used depends on the relative value of the commodities it has the capacity to produce. The highest amount someone would pay for the land is based on the most valuable economic use that is possible for the land.

Conservation easements involve the donation or sale of a property's development rights. In effect, a conservation easement separates the development rights from the land and then retires those rights by limiting how the land is used in the future. A conservation easement can be used to preserve ranching on the land. It can also be used to prohibit subdivision of the land. Or a conservation easement can be structured so that the landowner can reserve the right to develop a limited number of house sites, provided such development does not affect the land's conservation values. Often a portion of the income tax liability that results from the sale of a reserved house site can be offset by the charitable donation of the conservation easement. This may provide the rancher with additional liquidity. One of the attractive features of conservation easements is that they can be tailored to fit a specific property or to fit a specific landowner's financial circumstances or goals.

The value of the conservation easement gift for both the income tax deduction and the estate tax reduction is determined by a three-step appraisal. The first step is based on what the property would sell for if it were put to the most profitable economic use that is possible. For example, what is the highest amount someone would pay for the land if it were being bought for development? The second step is based on what the property would sell for after the conservation easement is placed on the land and the development rights are removed from it. For example, what is the highest amount someone would pay for the land if it were being bought to raise livestock? The value of the gift is equal to the difference between the value of the property *before* the conservation easement is granted, and the value of the property *after* the conservation easement is granted. The third step is to appraise the enhancement value. This is especially important "if the conservation easement does not cover all of the property owned by the donor or related parties, then any enhancement to the value of the excluded property (due to its adjacency to land protected by a conservation easement) is offset against the value of the conservation easement." It is critically important that a qualified appraiser with credible experience with conservation easements do the appraisal, because the appraisal is the document that is most likely to be reviewed by the IRS.

Federal Tax Law Incentives

Federal laws and IRS regulations provide income and estate tax incentives for land conservation. All of these are based on the idea that protecting certain lands serves the public good. The federally recognized conservation values include the natural habitat of fish, wildlife, or plants, historically important lands or structures, scenic views, and open space. The preservation of open space can include ranchland and forestland, when it is for the scenic enjoyment of the general public or when such preservation is in accordance with a conservation policy of the government for the benefit of the general public. Protection of these conservation values is the purpose of a conservation easement.

To qualify for federal tax benefits a "qualified conservation contribution" must be donated to a "qualified conservation organization" for "conservation purposes." The contribution must be an "easement or other interest in real property that under state law has attributes similar to an easement." The qualified conservation organization is either a charitable organization such as a land trust with 501(c)(3) status or a governmental entity. The conservation purposes include such things as habitat protection and open space preservation.

A tax deduction is not allowed if the easement protects one conservation value but permits the destruction of others.

A grantor of a conservation easement is allowed to deduct the value of the conservation easement from their federal income taxes with the following stipulation: the amount of the deduction cannot exceed 30 percent of the grantor's adjusted gross income (AGI) in the year of the gift and in each of the following five years. It is important to note that if the value of the conservation easement is substantially higher than the grantor's annual income, then the 30 percent limitation may make it impossible to take full advantage of the deduction.

Another option is to use a 50 percent limitation in one year for properties that have been owned for less than one year and are not considered a long-term capital gain property. This option seldom provides as much benefit as waiting one year and using the standard deduction schedule. The income tax benefits work differently for corporations—up to 10 percent of *taxable* income can be deducted each year for a total of six years. In all cases, get advice from a qualified financial and tax adviser.

For many ranchers, the lion's share of their net worth is tied up in the land. The primary tax benefit of granting a conservation easement for the land-rich and cash-poor rancher is lower estate taxes due to the reduced value of the estate to be taxed. However, in granting a conservation easement, it is possible for a grantor to reserve the right for a limited development. The sale of a few house sites may help to generate income for the land-rich and cash-poor rancher who may not otherwise have sufficient income to take full advantage of the potential income tax deduction. In this case the recording of the easement should be timed to coincide with the sale of the first house site in order to take full advantage of the six-year carryforward rule (30 percent AGI deducted from income taxes in the year of the gift and in each of the following five years). The income generated from the sale of the house sites may also be used to pay down debt so that the agricultural operation can begin to pay its own way.

The Income Tax Deduction

If a conservation easement satisfies the requirements of the Internal Revenue Code, then the grantor may receive an income tax deduction equal to the value of the conservation easement.

This income tax deduction may be applied against ordinary income as well as against income from capital gains.

Example 1: The ranch has been in the family for five generations. The current owners are in their early sixties. Discouraged by the declining cattle prices, the children decided not to go into ranching. The parents can't bear the idea of seeing the ranch sold and subdivided. Further, if the ranch is sold it will produce a hefty long-term capital gain. The parents decide to place a conservation easement on the ranch. The appraisal establishes that the ranch's fair market value (FMV) before the easement is $3,000,000, and that, after the easement, the value is $1,500,000. The value of the easement is $1,500,000 ($3,000,000–$1,500,000). For tax purposes the parents have reduced the value of the ranch by 50 percent and made a $1,500,000 charitable contribution. The parents have an adjusted gross income (AGI) of $50,000. They will be allowed to take a charitable deduction of up to 30 percent of their AGI or $15,000 (.30 x $50,000) in the year the gift is made and in each of the following five years. If their income remains the same for all six years, the total income tax deduction they will be allowed is $90,000 (6 x $15,000), leaving $1,410,000 of the allowable deduction unused.

Example 2: Same ranch, same family, and same facts as in Example 1. This time the conservation easement allows the sale of up to five house sites. Each site consists of a carefully located building envelope on a 10-acre lot. Further, each building envelope has been sited to ensure that no house is visible from any other house. The ranch's FMV after the easement that includes the right to develop the house sites is $1,700,000 rather than the $1,500,000 "after" value in Example 1. This is because the value of each lot is enhanced by $40,000 due to the protection afforded by the adjacent conservation easement (5 x $40,000 = $200,000). The value of the charitable contribution based on the "before" and "after" appraisals is now $1,300,000 ($3,000,000–$1,700,000). The lots sell for $250,000 each, and if one lot is sold each year the parents will have an AGI of $300,000 ($50,000+$250,000). They are allowed to take a charitable deduction of up to 30 percent of their AGI or $90,000 (.30 x $300,000) in the year the gift is made. They can carry the remaining $1,210,000 ($1,300,000–$90,000) forward for the next five years. If their income remains the same each year, they will be able to use a total of $540,000 of the allowable $1,300,000 deduction (6 years x $90,000 per year). With proper planning the ranch owners can structure the sale of the lots to allow for the maximum use of the allowable deduction within the six-year carryforward period. This can be accomplished by timing the sale of the lots or by financing the sale of the lots.

The Estate Tax Deduction

Granting a conservation easement not only protects your land from development, it also benefits your children by lowering the value of the land for estate tax purposes. According to Stephen J. Small, an attorney specializing in tax strategies for the landowner, the problem is this: "Without proper planning, a valuable piece of land in an estate can trigger an estate tax so large that the land itself will have to be sold to pay the estate tax." In the United States today, the highest effective federal estate tax rate is above 50 percent. As a result, according to Mr. Small, "for the first time in the history of the United States, the family that just wants to leave the land to the children may not be able to do that." The estate tax problem arises because land is valued for estate tax purposes at its maximum value for development (the highest density allowed under local law) even if the property has been used solely for ranching or agricultural purposes for decades or centuries.

For estate tax purposes, placing a conservation easement on a property results in a reduction in the land's value. Therefore, federal and state estate taxes are reduced. In effect a conservation easement removes part of the property's value from the estate.

The 1997 Taxpayer Relief Act added an additional incentive for landowners to donate a conservation easement. Called Section 2031(c) of the Internal Revenue Code, this new benefit allows the additional exclusion of 40 percent of the "after" value of the land subject to a conservation easement. The standard conservation easement tax rules still work the same way they did before the 1997 changes. The exclusion allowed by Section 2031(c) is *in addition* to any reduction in value that is the result of the restrictions already imposed on the land by the conservation easement under Section 170(h). With proper comprehensive planning, the new law allows an owner of important land to save many more estate tax dollars than was possible previously. As of 2002, the maximum amount that may be excluded from an estate under the new law is $500,000. This exclusion applies regardless of when the easement was donated. Also, according to Stephen J. Small, "if the planning is done correctly, the estates of both spouses can be eligible for the new Section 2031(c) exclusion."

To qualify for the Section 2031(c) exclusion, the conservation easement must prohibit all but minimal commercial recreational use of the land (*de minimis* use). It must also be donated by a member of the family that has owned the land for a minimum of three years. It is important to note that the exclusion does not apply to any development rights that have been reserved as part of the conservation easement. For example, the right to a limited development of house lots is a development right and, as such, will be subject to estate taxes. The right to continue ranching is not considered to be a development right, nor is the right to own and maintain an existing residence.

The Economic Growth and Tax Relief Reconciliation Act of 2001 changed the estate tax system by gradually phasing out and then repealing the estate tax in 2010 as follows:

Year	Estate tax exemption	Highest estate tax rate
2002	$1,000,000	50%
2003	$1,000,000	49%
2004	$1,500,000	48%
2005	$1,500,000	47%
2006	$2,000,000	46%

2007	$2,000,000	45%
2008	$2,000,000	45%
2009	$3,500,000	45%
2010	Estate tax repealed	Estate tax repealed

Congress must reenact the law by 2010 for the repeal of estate taxes to continue; otherwise the system reverts to the rates in effect before the act was signed. Until then, if a ranch is transferred from a deceased parent to the heirs, 2010 is the year to do it. In that year, the children would owe no estate taxes.

The following two examples illustrate how the changing estate tax exemption affects things.

Example 3: For this example the ranch, family, and facts remain the same as in Example 2 except that the last surviving owner dies in 2002, after placing a conservation easement on the ranch. The ranch's FMV is $3,000,000 *before* the conservation easement and $1,500,000 *after* the easement. The estate tax that would have been due on the ranch had no easement been placed on the ranch is $780,000. To find this number subtract the $1,000,000 exemption and apply the applicable tax (39%) on the remaining $2,000,000. The estate tax that is due on the ranch with the easement is approximately $155,000. To find this number subtract the $1,000,000 exemption and apply the applicable tax (31%) on the remaining $500,000 (1,500,000–1,000,000 = 500,000 x .31 = 155,000). The family saves $625,000 (780,000 –155,000) in estate taxes as a result of the conservation easement.

Under the 1997 Taxpayer's Relief Act, if the easement is a "qualified conservation easement" an additional $500,000 (40% of 1,500,000 up to a maximum of 500,000) may be excluded from the estate taxes. Combined with the $1,000,000 exemption and this $500,000 exclusion, the conservation easement eliminates the estate tax, a savings to the family of $780,000.

Example 4: Same family and facts except the last parent dies in 2004. Now, the conservation easement "takedown" results in the entire remaining $1,500,000 estate being exempt from estate taxes. There is no need to invoke the additional 40 percent reduction. *The heirs pay no estate taxes at all*. Clean and simple. In the coming years, this kind of estate tax relief may become a major factor in keeping ranches in the family whether or not a conservation easement is granted. But for those ranchers who want to see their place stay undeveloped, a conservation easement will remain the tool of choice.

Property Tax Reduction

There is usually no reduction in property taxes when a conservation easement is put on a ranch. In most states, agricultural property is already taxed at the lowest rate. In some states, land is assessed on its potential for development and an easement might bring relief. The landowner needs competent advice on the state property tax laws to see if taxes can be reduced.

Get Good Advice

The advice of an attorney or accountant familiar with the latest federal and state tax laws is vital. The preceding examples illustrate general cases only.

A conservation easement is a legal instrument that allows the landowner to combine saving land with saving taxes. The gift of a conservation easement offers one of those rare opportunities in life of being able to do well by doing good. It is an opportunity to take back control of the destiny of your ranch because, if you don't plan what to do with your land, the federal government is going to tell you what to do with your land—sell it to pay the taxes. Although other methods exist for reducing estate tax burdens, only a conservation easement results in the protection of a property from development. By voluntarily giving up the land's conservation values on your own terms, you can safeguard your most important asset and your family from the destructive impact of estate taxes. And you leave a legacy of land for your children.

Ponderosa Pine, Montosa Ranch.

9 Case Studies

Conservation easements are a highly flexible tool that can meet the needs of a broad range of landowners. Landowners who have income to shelter may choose to donate an easement of their entire property. For financial reasons, other ranchers may need to exclude some land from the easement or draft the easement to allow for the limited development of a certain number of lots. Developers may use conservation easements as a component of an overall master plan for a property. The designs of conservation easements vary widely. Figure 9.1 illustrates three of the variations that are discussed as case studies in this chapter.

In all cases, the protection of significant conservation resources is the key. Easements donated on undevelopable land with no particular environmental or open space importance will generate few (if any) tax benefits and are a fundamental misuse of the device. Land trusts should not accept these "abusive" easements—to do so would be to jeopardize the land trust's tax-exempt status, its reputation, and the reputation of the entire land trust community. A proper conservation easement is the charitable gift of development rights on important land, which could otherwise be lost to development.

The following case studies explore three ways that easements are being used in the West.

- Basic Ranch Easements: two examples of conservation easements that reserve a few family homesites.
- Regional Cooperation: one example of regional cooperation among ranchers using conservation easements along the Blackfoot River.

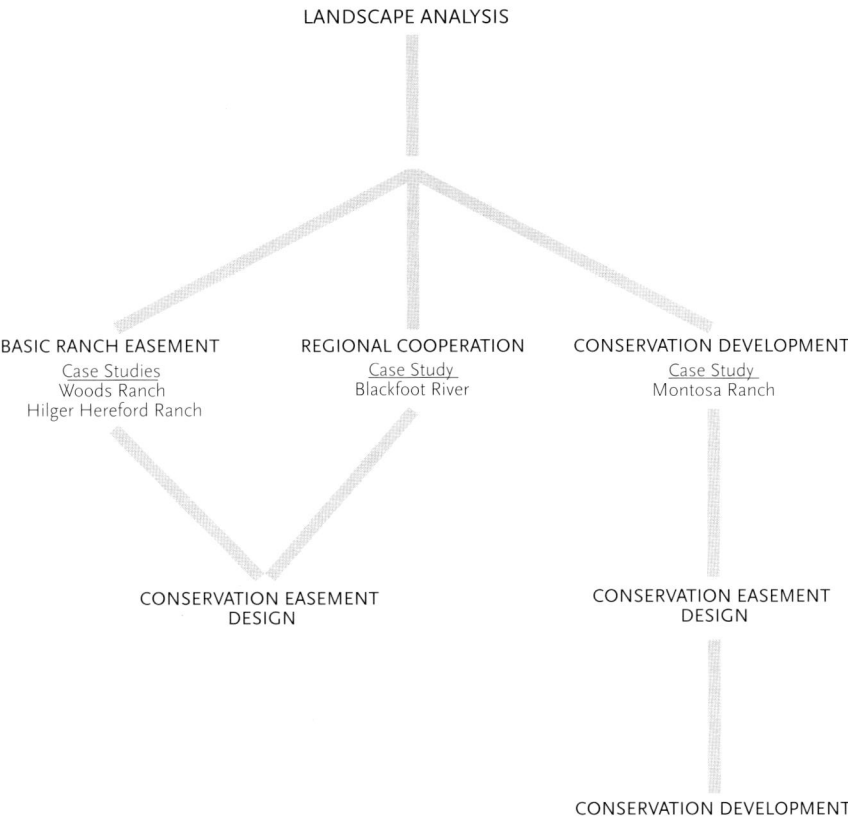

Figure 9.1 | Conservation Easement Variations

- Conservation Development: One example of a conservation easement including a limited, protective development of large lots on the Montosa Ranch, which is designed to realize the landowners' financial goals while protecting the integrity of the ranch.

Basic Ranch Easements

"Woods Ranch"

The "Woods Ranch" conservation easement demonstrates how these projects work. This hypothetical example combines typical design elements (see Figure 9.2).

The Woods Ranch places a conservation easement on the entire ranch with only a few family homesites reserved for future development. This is the most common type of easement in the West. Hundreds of examples exist. The main goal is to keep the property open and in ranching with a few homesites reserved for family members and/or a lot held back for sale.

The ranch is owned by a couple in their sixties with a son and a daughter who want to keep ranching when they inherit the place. A local land trust was contacted, family discussions were held, and the couple went ahead with a donated conservation easement. Their goals were to keep the place in production, allow homesites for the two kids to raise their families on, and hold back a 50-acre tract for sale to raise cash.

A conservation easement was designed that prohibited subdivision and development of most of the ranch. A "development area" or "building envelope" was created around the existing ranch headquarters as part of the conservation easement. The son and daughter will build their homes there. A 50-acre parcel was held out of the easement where another home could be built. The remaining land was protected by a conservation easement. Forest management areas were mapped where thinning for disease control and fire prevention can occur. Limited commercial selective logging was allowed in line with a separate Forest Management Plan. Floodplain forests could still be grazed but no cutting of trees could occur within 50 yards of a great blue heron nesting area—something the ranchers agreed to because they loved watching the big birds fly over the place. The family left open the possibility of working with the state fish and game agency to reintroduce river otters to Odell Creek. A commercial gravel pit was excluded from the easement because the Woods family needed the revenue it provided.

Ranch management, including a designated "cropland" area, was left up to the owners except for a restriction on aerial spraying of biocides. No public access is allowed on the ranch —same as before. Restrictions on cell phone towers, landing strips, golf courses, billboards, and other land use changes were also included in the easement. The final product ended up keeping the place more or less as is except for the three allowed homes.

The Woods Ranch easement was recorded and continues to be in force despite the death of the parents. The two heirs now run cow–calf pairs, grow grain, thin the timber, irrigate, spray the weeds, and enjoy a ranching way of life. The 50-acre parcel was sold for $400,000— money that helped create a financial reserve for the ranch operation. Once a year someone from the trust comes by at a scheduled time to drive across the ranch and take photos at the photo points shown in the baseline report. No "violations" have occurred, and the relationship between the ranchers and land trust is cordial. The Woods heirs have talked to their neighbors, and three other ranch families have now protected their property along the Kinte River with similar easements.

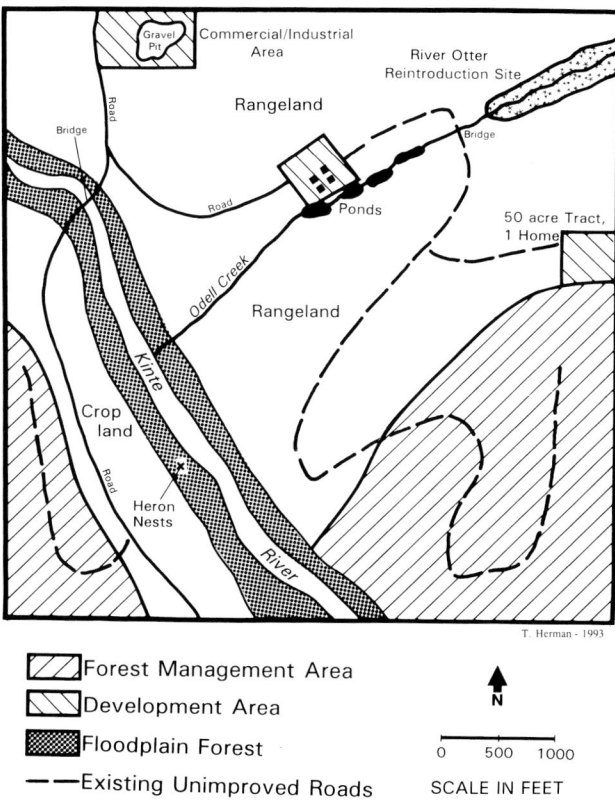

Figure 9.2 | "Woods Ranch": This case study is a hypothetical example that combines typical design elements.

Hilger Hereford Ranch

The Hilger Hereford Ranch in central Montana stands out as a strong example of the power of easements to fulfill the wishes of ranch families. This project was completed in 1984 with the Montana Land Reliance and is still protecting the place today. The roots of the deal go back decades.

The owners were four elderly, unmarried siblings: Bryan, Dan, Susan, and Babe Hilger. Their property had been in the family since before Montana was a state. This magnificent cattle ranch was covered with cottonwood bottomlands, hay ground, bunchgrass prairies, and pine forests. Elk, deer, and pronghorns depended on it. Mountain lions, coyotes, black bears, and badgers hunted the meadows. Waterfowl covered the lake each spring and fall. The Missouri River passed through—a national class trout fishery right out the front door.

In July 1805, Lewis and Clark paddled up the Missouri toward what would become the Hilger Hereford Ranch. Through the din of a hailstorm, Meriwether Lewis watched as the bedrock wall appeared to part like the gates of a fortress as the river entered the ridgelines:

> The rocks approach the river on both sides forming the most sublime and extraordinary spectacle. We have entered the most remarkable cliffs that we have yet seen. These cliffs rise from the water's edge to the height of 1200 feet. The river seems to have forced its way through this immense body of solid rock for the distance of five and three-quarters miles. From the singular appearance of this place, I called it The Gates of The Mountains.

Then Lewis described the site of the future Hilger Hereford Ranch: "Here the perpendicular rocks cease, the hills retire from the river and the valley widens to a greater extent than it has done since we entered the mountains." Lewis also noted a large spring pouring from the ground. This was the future spot of a homestead cabin built in 1867 by a twenty-six-year-old immigrant from Luxembourg named Nicholas Hilger.

Hilger ranched the place and thrived. He even found time to serve as a Justice of the Peace in Helena. In 1886, he had a solid steel steamboat built—*The Rose of Helena*—to haul tourists to see the Gates of the Mountains. President William Henry Harrison was one of the sightseers. By 1906, the *Rose* was beached and left to rust. Its boiler still lies on the ranch.

In 1908, Hauser Dam was built across the Missouri upstream from the ranch. The earthen dam soon burst, unleashing a 30-foot wall of water. Dan Hilger, his mother, and the other kids jumped onto a buckboard and slapped leather for high ground. They barely escaped. Their house was picked up by the surge, floated into a large eddy, and was eventually dumped. When the family entered the house by rowboat, they found a fencepost sticking through the kitchen floor, a lighted lantern floating in the hall, and a full sugar bowl perched in a hall-mounted candleholder. The Hilgers shrugged, repaired the house, and moved back in.

Nicholas Hilger Jr. began operating the ranch out of a new stone home. Everyone just called him "N.D." A herd of four hundred cattle were grazed on the property. His children—Bryan, Dan, Susan, and Babe—acquired 640-acre homesteads and purchased more land from neighbors who sold out during the droughts of the late teens and early 1920s. N.D. started the boat tours back up with a vessel called *The Rose of Helena II* until the Great Depression halted things for good. Then even the ranch business got hard.

For one brief stretch, N.D. lost the ranch to the bankers, but the four kids quickly got it back. After N.D. passed away, the Hilgers turned their energy toward raising purebred Polled Herefords. They got good at it, breeding superb Benchmark Dams like Hilger Mode Sara and Coppertone Sara F—animals capable of producing the finest calves in the region. Dozens of bulls, such as Hilger Special 415, became Grand Champions. The Hilgers raised and sold thirty solid bulls a year. This provided a steady and sufficient living. Ranch debt became a thing of the past.

The Hilger Hereford Ranch supported three generations of ranchers. The family has toughed it out through everything imaginable, including drought, flood, fire, economic depression, and loneliness. And still the land is in superb shape.

The Hilgers donated a conservation easement to the Montana Land Reliance to make sure it stays that way. No new homesites are allowed—only buildings at the ranch headquarters. The easement was straightforward with no frills. The goal was to keep the place like it is—a working cattle ranch. With no heirs, the Hilgers sold the place to a young ranch family and retained a life estate so they could spend their last years on the place they loved.

Dan Hilger spoke one day out by the stone house. The building was crowded with ox-yokes, horseshoes, butter churns, farm equipment, and old tack. It gave the day the scent of history. Dan looked around and explained why they had donated the easement:

> We were getting too old to do all the ranch work. I couldn't help with the cattle. Babe was getting too old and I couldn't do it all myself. People started coming out of the woodwork, long-lost, shirttail relatives showing up, letters from interested buyers, real estate agents; everyone wanted to buy the Hilger Ranch. But we didn't want the ranch spoiled. That's why we threw in with the Montana Land Reliance people. The conservation easement guarantees that Hilger land will never be subdivided and whoever buys the ranch down the line is still covered by that deal. That land across the river isn't under a conservation easement. There's several houses on it now and it's gonna get worse; about seventy lots are laid out. They call them estates or something.

But that can never happen on the Hilger Hereford Ranch. It will produce beef and beauty forever. So will the ranch next door. The Carrie Hilger Ranch is now also protected by a conservation easement with the Montana Land Reliance, a group that now holds 515 easements covering over 500,000 agricultural acres.

Today, none of the Hilgers are still with us, but their wishes are still being honored. Drive by the ranch these days and you'll see good grass and thick cow bellies. It will always be so. A family with deep roots in Montana made a decision that we can all be grateful for. They chose to save the ranch.

Regional Cooperation

The Blackfoot River Valley

The Blackfoot River Valley in western Montana is the setting of one of the West's most successful conservation easement programs. During the 1960s, ranchlands along the Blackfoot began to disappear into recreational subdivisions. Productive ranches and the wildlife habitats and scenic views they provided were being lost. At the same time, the popularity of the river with floaters and anglers grew rapidly. As the landscape changed, local ranchers and other landowners figured they'd seen enough. Over cups of coffee at the Sunset Hill School a list of choices began to take shape. About all everybody agreed on was that the valley had to be saved.

The possibility of having the Blackfoot declared a Wild and Scenic River was rejected. No one wanted a heavy federal hand involved. Zoning and other land use regulations were seen as cumbersome, ineffective, and just plain awful. The ranchers wouldn't be told what to do with their land.

Conservation easements were introduced in the 1970s as an alternative. This voluntary, compensating alternative was well received. A 30-mile-long stretch of the river was agreed on where interested landowners would be worked with. If you didn't want to hear about easements, no one came knocking. At first, the idea was to complete several easements at the same time. Each would be negotiated, prepared, held by an escrow agent, and then filed on the same day so neighbors could be sure everyone was fully committed. Some ranchers figured, "I'll only do it when everyone else does." The escrow system would cover everyone's back.

It didn't turn out that way. Since every family confronts estate tax obligations and financial ups and downs at different times, the easements ended up coming in one by one.

Edna Brunner went first. In 1974, she and her son Paul saved a riverside ranch.

When good word of mouth spread about the project, other landowners lined up to donate easements.

The 5 Star Double R Ranch came next. Fanny Steele owned the place. She was a champion bucking horse rider and had been in movies with Rudy Vallee and Monte Montana. Her specialty was standing up on the backside of a galloping mare—facing backward—twirling lassos in both hands. Old movie posters and flyers from sixty-year-old rodeos covered a long splintered table in one of her sheds.

Then came the Blackwood Ranch—a nice spread for purebred cattle that was covered with glacial potholes full of ducks.

Next was the Monture Hereford Ranch—3,656 acres. Cora Barbour's place. One of the best outfits in the valley.

Otto and Jenny Eder ran a 1,280-acre spread that was prized by local realtors. They chose to donate an easement instead and make a steady living from cattle and a bit of forest thinning.

The Lindbergh Cattle Company donated two easements covering 3 miles of the Blackfoot River on both sides. Land Lindbergh ran cattle, cut hay from irrigated circles, and fished when he got a chance. He helped lead the effort to get the word out.

In all cases, the conservation easement restrictions focused on subdivision, mining, industrial facilities, and other major land uses while leaving ranch management alone.

Some ranchers went early, some went late, a few preferred not to go at all. The stories mounted up as easements were donated along the Blackfoot. But the recreational use still had to be dealt with because the river was attracting hundreds of people to fish and float every summer weekend.

The ranchers understood that trespassing would only get worse unless they took control. They accomplished this not by buckshot and bigger signs but by allowing controlled river access at a few carefully chosen sites. No landowner was in any way required to allow public use. The state fish and game agency would manage this with help from the county. Ranchers and public agencies signed a separate recreation management agreement—completely independent of the conservation easement. The rules were posted all over the watershed: a few marked parking places were allowed at the river's edge, trash must be picked up, fires were banned, poachers would be arrested, and anyone caught trespassing outside of the specific river access sites would be prosecuted. Everyone agreed that if the public ran roughshod over the rules, the landowners could terminate the agreement. At first, everyone signed up for just one year. When the ranchers felt that worked out well, they signed a five-year agreement. Today, river use is managed under a ten-year agreement and conflicts are rare.

Today, over 35,000 acres have been placed under easement within the Blackfoot River drainage. The Montana Land Reliance, Five Valleys Land Trust, and The Nature Conservancy have accepted donated easements from ranchers, ranch corporations, retirees, and other landowners. Each landowner chooses who they want to do business with.

These ranches were saved through the independent actions of dozens of individuals. But it took cooperation and a willingness to listen to make those actions work together to create a better future for everyone. The Blackfoot River Valley shows what can happen when conservation easements are used to maintain a ranching landscape people love and respect.

Conservation Development

The Montosa Ranch Project

The Montosa Ranch straddles the northeastern edge of the Plains of San Agustín west of Magdalena, New Mexico (see Figure 9.3). The Plains are an ancient lakebed, and over millennia prevailing southwestern winds have carried its silt onto the ranch. As a result, the soils on the ranch consist of silt loam and loamy sand with an effective rooting depth of 60 inches or more. Runoff is slow, and the hazard of water erosion is slight. Characteristic grasses are black grama, sideoats grama, blue grama, western wheatgrass, and bottlebrush squirreltail. Parts of the ranch are distinguished by an abundance of ponderosa pine in addition to piñon pine and juniper. Typically, ponderosa pine is found only in areas with more than 18 inches of annual precipitation. On average the Montosa Ranch receives between 12 and 15 inches. The sandy soil's capacity to retain water makes up for the shortfall.

Figure 9.3 | **Montosa Ranch Aerial Overview**: The Montosa Ranch straddles the northeastern edge of the Plains of San Agustín, west of Magdalena, New Mexico. Aerial photo/mapping: Thomas R. Mann and Associates/Bohannan Huston, Inc.

B.W. Cox, co-owner and manager of the Montosa Ranch. Photo: Anthony Anella.

"This old country promises less and delivers more than any country I've ever been in," says B.W. Cox, the managing owner of the Montosa Ranch. "It is because of the sand."

B.W. Cox is a connoisseur of nature. He knows the relationship between the wind-borne sediments from an ancient lakebed and his ranch's capacity for growing grass. He knows how the wind has shaped the growth of trees over time and how the forms of the trees indicate where to seek shelter from the wind. He knows where the sun melts the snow first and the location of the warmest places on the ranch for calving. He knows that to continue ranching he must respect the delicate balance between rainfall and the land's capacity to support livestock without overgrazing. He also knows that the secret to gleaning a living from land in the arid West is water. B.W. has installed more than 500,000 linear feet of PVC pipe to supply watering tubs he has scattered throughout the ranch. The pipeline connects a system of five wells with a network of more than eighty watering tubs that allow the cattle to spread out and graze the entire ranch. B.W. recycles tractor tires to make the watering tubs. He has found that the black rubber not only acts as an insulator, it also absorbs solar energy. As a result, water does not freeze as solidly as it does in the cold metal of a steel trough. It is these kinds of insights that make B.W. a successful rancher. He understands that the ecology of ranching has to do with an interaction between soil, water, wind, sun, vegetation, and human beings. B.W.'s livelihood depends on his astute ability to read the land and on his ability to work with nature, not against it.

B.W. and his wife Billie grew up on ranches near Young, Arizona, and Douglas, Arizona, respectively. In 1954, when they married, B.W.'s first job was breaking horses for a ranch owned by the San Carlos Apache Tribe near Globe. For thirty-eight years, first his father and then B.W. managed the immense Red Lake Ranch near Acoma Pueblo in New Mexico. During that time Billie and their two sons lived in Magdalena so the boys could go to school, while B.W. stayed on the ranch tending to the cattle. In 1981, B.W. had a "horse wreck" and had to be flown by helicopter to Albuquerque where he spent three months recovering in a hospital. B.W. and Billie thought their ranching days were over, and B.W. spent the next seven years working as a ranch appraiser for a bank in Belen, New Mexico. During that time B.W. acquired an understanding of real estate financing to complement his practical understanding of ranching. Seven years later, B.W. had healed, and he and Billie were able to return to ranching. In 1989, B.W. and Billie Cox bought the Montosa Ranch with a lifelong friend and California industrialist. The ranch consists of approximately 32,000 deeded acres and approximately 40,000 acres of land leased from the U.S. Forest Service and State of New Mexico.

Now in their late sixties, both B.W. and Billie are interested in setting up trusts for their two sons. One son, Roland, has a physical handicap that prevents him from managing the ranch. The other son, Lynn, lives in Albuquerque with his wife, and is not interested in ranching. Because their wealth is tied up in land, B.W. and Billie realized that to accomplish their financial goals, they would have to subdivide part of the ranch to get out some of their equity. At first they looked at developing approximately 2,000 acres into 20- to 40-acre lots. However, they decided against this approach. The idea of having that many new neighbors did not sit well. They also did not want to see the kind of subdivision of their land that is being developed around Datil, New Mexico, located 25 miles away on the other side of the Plains of San Agustín. Both B.W. and Billie have an emotional attachment to ranching as a way of life. They want to live out their lives on the Montosa Ranch. When the idea of a conservation easement development was first presented to B.W., he was hesitant to consider it. The word "perpetuity" scared him.

"I don't have all the answers for the best way to manage the ranch for the future," B.W. said at the time, "but I want to keep my options open. Forever is a long time. I don't want to be cursed by future generations for a wrongheaded decision I may make today."

Gathering calves for branding, Montosa Ranch. 2003.
Photo: Anthony Anella.

Flanking a calf for branding, Montosa Ranch. 2003.
Photo: Anthony Anella.

Although he has a very different financial profile, B.W. and Billie's partner in the ranch was also reluctant to consider the use of a conservation easement. He had not heard of conservation easements before, but they sounded a lot like "tree hugging" to him. Fortunately for the project, the ranch's attorney, John Garrett, was open to the idea of a conservation easement. "Why be against it," John asked, "if it can satisfy your financial goals, and do some greater good?"

Two critical questions emerged for the owners: How do you maximize the fair market value of a limited number of lots that will be adequate to realize your financial goals without also providing open space amenities to the prospective lot buyers? And how do you develop a limited number of lots in a way that will not adversely affect the ranch and the ranching way of life you enjoy?

It turns out that these two questions are different sides of the same equation. Like most ranchers, B.W. and Billie Cox are not interested in seeing their land subdivided. On the other side, most conservation buyers are not interested in running a ranch. They value the land for the scenery, recreational opportunities, and privacy afforded by open space. Conservation easement design and development balances both sides of the equation. On one side it allows the ranch owners a way to get some equity out of the land while at the same time it preserves the integrity of the land for ranching. On the other side it protects the conservation values of the land that make it attractive to the conservation buyer. It also protects the conservation values that are required to qualify for the income and estate tax benefits.

Although the owners were reluctant to place a conservation easement on the entire ranch, they recognized the need to enhance the value of the lots by protecting the views from the house sites. They worked with Conservation Design Partners, an Albuquerque-based group that specializes in environmentally sensitive development. Conservation Design Partners asked David Ater and Leon Mellow, two Santa Fe–based real estate brokers, to consult on the early stages of the project. The realtors pointed out that "unless the buyer perceives that the exclusivity being offered is legally assured in perpetuity, the pricing being considered will not hold up. Therefore, it is essential that the entire land plan be confirmed and the extent of the conservation easement be decided before the lots are put on the market." Conservation Design Partners also asked Tracy Conner, a Santa Fe–based attorney who specializes in conservation easements, to help analyze the financial and tax implications of several different scenarios for the landowners to consider. Using hypothetical numbers, the scenarios were based on the following assumptions:

Three generations of the Saulsberry family branding calves, Montosa Ranch. 2003. Photo: Anthony Anella.

- Total area of ranch: 32,000 deeded acres
- Total area of lots to be sold: 5,000 deeded acres
- Total area of viewshed as seen from lots: 5,000 deeded acres
- Total area of ranch headquarters: 5,000 deeded acres
- BEFORE value of ranch, unencumbered by easement: $150/acre
- AFTER value of ranch, easement encumbering all of ranch: $75/acre
- Value of lots, if lots and entire ranch are under easement: $400/acre
- Value of lots, if entire ranch but not lots are under easement: $500/acre
  (Note: Value increases because of potential tax benefit to buyer.)

- Value of lots, if only lots and viewshed are under easement: $300/acre
  (Note: Value decreases because less land is being protected.)
- Enhancement of portion of ranch not under easement: $50/acre

Scenario One

Entire ranch, including seven lots and ranch headquarters, is placed under a conservation easement. 32,000 acres.

Before value ($150/acre):	$4,800,000
After value ($75/acre):	$2,400,000
Easement value:	$2,400,000
Sale price of lots ($400/acre):	$2,000,000

Scenario Two

Ranch, excluding lots (5,000 acres) and ranch headquarters (5,000 acres), is placed under a conservation easement. 32,000 acres–10,000 acres = 22,000 acres.

Before value (22,000 acres):	$3,300,000
After value (22,000 acres):	$1,650,000
Easement value:	$1,650,000
Less enhancement	
(10,000 acres):	($ 500,000)
Easement value:	$1,150,000
Sale price of lots ($500/acre*):	$2,500,000

---

* Value of lots increases to $500/acre because of potential tax benefit to buyer who would donate a conservation easement on their land.

Scenario Three

Ranch, excluding ranch headquarters (5,000 acres), is placed under a conservation easement. 32,000 acres–5,000 acres = 27,000 acres.

Before value (27,000 acres):	$4,050,000
After value (27,000 acres):	$2,025,000
Easement value:	$2,025,000
Less enhancement (5,000 acres):	($ 250,000)
Easement value:	$1,775,000
Sale price of lots ($400/acre):	$2,000,000

Scenario Four

Only seven lots (5,000 acres) and viewshed (5,000 acres) are placed under a conservation easement. Total: 10,000 acres.

Before value (10,000 acres):	$1,500,000
After value (10,000 acres):	$ 750,000
Easement value:	$ 750,000
Less enhancement (22,000 acres):	($1,100,000)
Easement value:	($ 350,000)
Sale price of lots ($300/acre*):	$1,500,000

---

* Value of lots decreases to $300/acre because of less land being protected.

In this scenario the easement donation ends up having no value due to the enhancement of the value of the part of the ranch that is not placed under the easement.

Scenario Five

Only the viewshed (5,000 acres) is placed under a conservation easement.
32,000 acres–5,000 acres = 27,000 acres.

Before value (5,000 acres):	$ 750,000
After value (5,000 acres):	$ 375,000
Easement value:	$ 375,000
Less enhancement	
(27,000 acres):	($1,350,000)
Easement value:	($ 975,000)
Sale price of lots ($300/acre*):	$1,500,000

* Value of lots decreases to $300/acre because of less land being protected.

In this scenario the easement donation also ends up having no value due to the enhancement of the value of the part of the ranch that is not placed under the easement.

As the owners evaluated the different scenarios, four factors influenced their decision-making process:

- The desire to maximize the fair market value of the limited number of lots to be sold.
- The desire to maximize the tax deduction.
- The amount of land to be encumbered by the easement.
- The restrictions on land use that would be required by the easement.

Scenario One illustrates how placing the entire ranch under the easement maximizes the value of the easement. However, this approach does not allow the ranch owners to "hedge their bets." What if they were wrong about conservation easements? They decided against this scenario.

Scenario Two illustrates how placing most of the ranch—but not the lots—under the easement maximizes the fair market value of the lots. The advantage of not placing the lots under the conservation easement prior to the sale is that it may help the prospective buyer to justify a higher purchase price because of subsequent tax benefits that would come from their placing a conservation easement on the lot. The disadvantage of this approach is that it depends on trust between the buyer and the seller that the buyer will place a conservation easement on the lot. There can be no formal legal agreement without negating the potential tax benefits to the buyer. This is because the conservation easement has to be voluntarily donated to obtain the tax benefits; the IRS would disallow a quid pro quo. There could be no guarantee that the lot buyer would not subdivide the lot, which was precisely what the ranch owners were trying to avoid. The possibility of placing restrictive covenants on the lots as a way of preventing the buyers from further subdividing the lots (without having to rely on trust) was also explored. However, restrictive covenants depend on private individuals for enforcement. The ranch owners did not want to worry about these potential legal costs. And if the restrictive covenants were enforced by injunction as part of the deed, there would be no tax benefits to the lot buyer for placing a conservation easement on the lots because the lots would already be protected from future subdivision by the deed restriction. For these reasons, the ranch owners decided against this scenario.

Grama grass, Montosa Ranch.

Case Studies 123

Clearing Piñon Pine and Juniper to create more pasture and generate income from the sale of firewood, Montosa Ranch.

Scenario Three illustrates how placing most of the ranch—including the lots but not the ranch headquarters—under the easement provides a compromise solution. The sale price of the lots being sold under the easement is less than the example of Scenario Two, but there is no uncertainty about what will happen to the lots: The conservation easement prevents further subdivision. Further, it is the land trust's responsibility to enforce the terms of the conservation easement. The ranch owners do not have to worry about the potential legal costs for enforcement. And by keeping the ranch headquarters out of the easement, the ranch owners are not restricted from developing this land. They can hedge their bets.

Scenario Three also illustrates how keeping only a small portion of the ranch out of the easement results in only a small reduction in the easement value for tax purposes due to the "enhancement value." In contrast, Scenarios Four and Five both illustrate how the easement donation ends up having no value (*and might actually result in a tax liability*) when too much land is left unencumbered by the easement. The enhancement value derives from the fact that land adjacent to protected land becomes more valuable than land adjacent to unprotected land. The IRS requires an accounting of this added value for the landowner in calculating the donation value of the conservation easement. Therefore, the donation value of the conservation easement is determined by subtracting the enhancement value of the land kept out of the easement from the fair market value of the easement.

In the end the owners decided on Scenario Three: to place most of the ranch—27,000 of the 32,000 deeded acres—under a conservation easement. The conservation easement includes the seven 640-acre lots that are to be sold. Under the terms of the conservation easement, each lot has the reserved right to fence a 5-acre development area and a 5-acre pasture area. The lot buyer is allowed to graze only a limited number of horses in the pasture. No fencing of the 640-acre-lot boundaries is allowed, and the ranch owners retain the right to graze the lots outside of the 10 acres each lot buyer is allowed to fence. All buildings and other disturbances to the landscape must be located within the 5-acre development area. Further, the principal residence is restricted to a specific building envelope.

The building envelopes were located using the sieve mapping design process (see Figures 9.4–9.14). Those portions of the ranch that fell through the design "sieve" of protected land were considered appropriate for development as potential house sites. Within those areas, the potential house sites were analyzed in terms of wind protection, solar access, and views (see Figures 9.15–9.19). Finally, to ensure that no lot owner would see the house of a neighbor, helium-filled balloons were tethered at each proposed house site to test the visibility of each house site from any of the others.

The 640-acre lot size was based on what A.C. Taylor, the realtor responsible for marketing the project, considered to be marketable. The model can be modified to fit different marketing circumstances. It works equally well with 50-acre lots. Whether the lot is 50 acres or 640 acres, the lot buyer can build only within a specific building envelope.

From a marketing point of view, Scenario Three also makes the most sense, given the owners' understandable reluctance to encumber the entire ranch with a conservation easement. A.C. Taylor pointed out that what is being sold is not so much real estate as a package of amenities consisting of protected open space, and that placing most if not all of the ranch under a conservation easement created a much better package to sell.

Equally important from the realtors' point of view was for the prospective buyer to understand the conservation and ranching aspects of the deal. The Montosa Ranch is a *working* cattle ranch. The continued operation of the ranch needs to be protected as a reserved right, including, for example, grazing rights as well as the right to construct fences, corrals, water wells, pipelines, and the like.

The fact that in Scenario Three the lots are included as part of the conservation easement BEFORE the lots are sold is significant. This is because the conservation easement helps to define exactly what is being sold. The owners wanted the building site restrictions (the precise locations of the building sites, the development areas, and the pasture areas) to be included in the conservation easement and they wanted the conservation easement to be recorded before the sale of the first lot so that the restrictions could not become negotiating points with

Piñon Pine and Juniper firewood, Montosa Ranch.

Figure 9.4 | **Natural Drainage:** This overlay corresponds to land located within 150 feet on either side of an arroyo or natural drainage system. This land is being protected from development in order to preserve the natural drainage pattern of the land and to provide habitat for wildlife.

Figure 9.5 | **Nonbuildable Peaks:** This overlay corresponds to land located on ridges or peaks down to 40-contour-feet below the tops of the ridge or peak. This land is being protected from development in order to keep the natural horizon free from human-made structures.

Figure 9.6 | **Wells and Water Lines:** This overlay corresponds to land located within a 300-foot radius of stock tanks. It also denotes the location of existing waterlines. This land is being protected from development because of the critical importance of water wells and stock tanks both to the operation of the Montosa Ranch as a working cattle ranch and to wildlife.

9.4

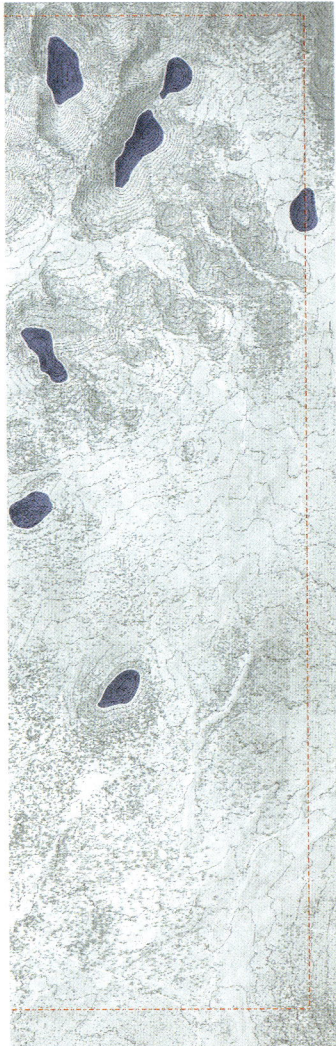

9.5

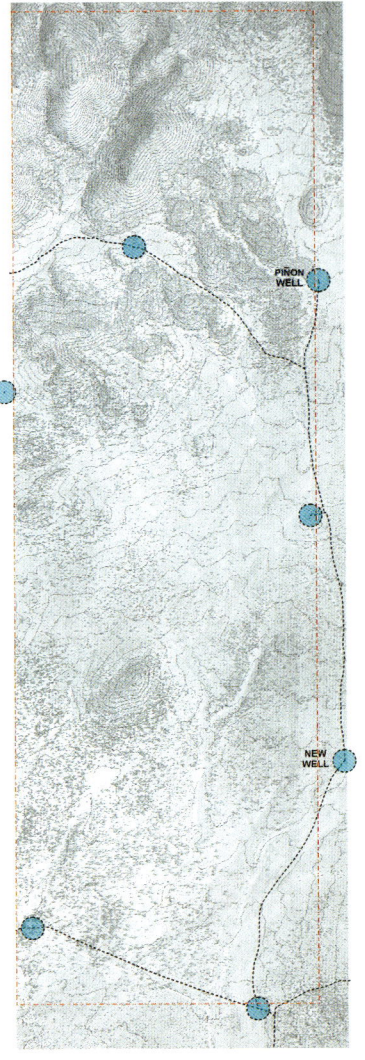

9.6

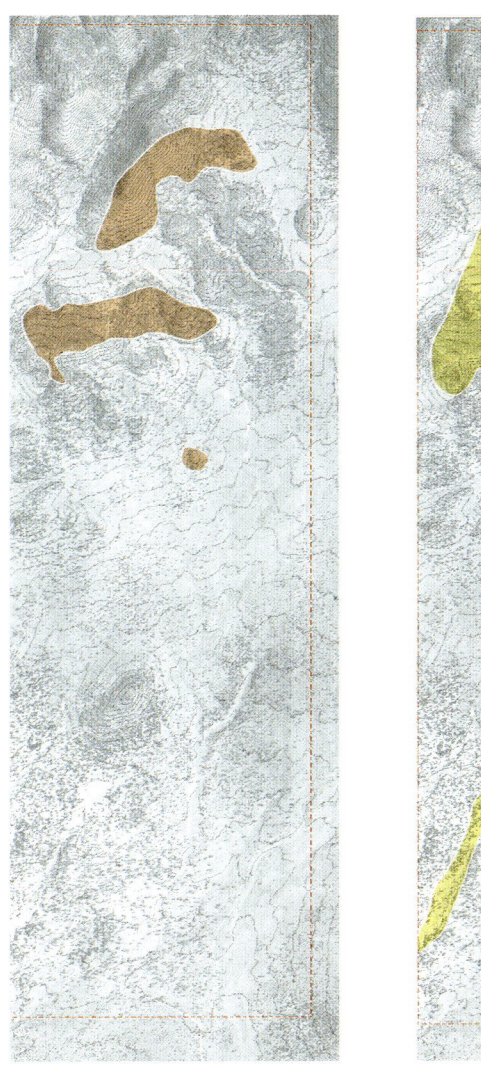

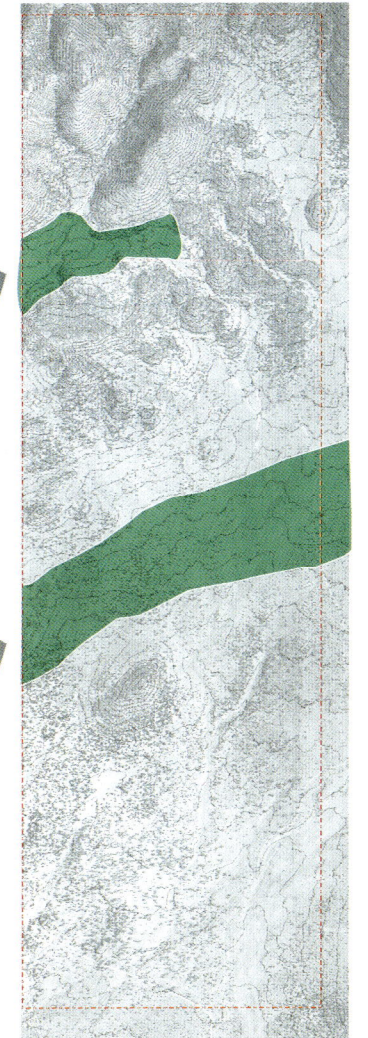

Figure 9.7 | Archaeological Sites: This overlay corresponds to areas where there are concentrations of archaeological sites. This land is being protected from development in order to preserve the cultural heritage left by previous inhabitants.

Figure 9.8 | Elk Habitat: This overlay corresponds to known corridors of elk migration as well as to prime elk habitat. It is based on information provided by the outfitter who leads hunts on the ranch, and by the ranch owner. This land is being protected from development in order to preserve elk habitat and migration routes.

Figure 9.9 | "Blowsand" Zone: This overlay corresponds to areas where sand has been blown in from the Plains of San Agustín. The location of the sand is an indicator of the prevailing wind pattern over geologic time. This land is being protected from development in order to avoid building houses in zones of high wind as evidenced by the sand.

9.7   9.8   9.9

Case Studies 127

Figure 9.10 | Steep Slopes: This overlay corresponds to the land where the slope exceeds 25 percent. This land is being protected from development to prevent erosion damage due to building on steep slopes.

the prospective buyers. The owners knew that if the restrictions were included only in the covenants, the savvy prospective buyer would know that the owners could modify the covenants for the sake of a sale.

However, monitoring the building site restrictions as part of a conservation easement is a responsibility that not all land trusts will accept. From the land trust's point of view, this responsibility adds to the risk of having to defend the conservation easement in court. For this reason, the initial land trust involved decided to pull out of the project. As a new land trust just getting started, it was honest about its limited capacity to monitor and enforce such restrictions. The New Mexico Land Conservation Collaborative (NMLCC) had more experience with easements that included building site restrictions. The NMLCC board was willing to accept the responsibility of monitoring and enforcing the building site restrictions as part of the conservation easement. To facilitate the land trust's monitoring and enforcement responsibilities, the ranch owners had the building sites, the 5-acre development areas, and the 5-acre pasture areas surveyed and staked. Doing this reduced the potential for any misunderstanding of the conservation easement by the lot buyers: they know up-front where they can build and what they can fence. To further strengthen the land trust's capacity to monitor and enforce the conservation easement, the amount of the stewardship contribution was tied to the number of lots that were actually sold. Since each lot buyer represents a potential lawsuit, this formula made sense for the land trust. It also made sense for the ranch owners, who could defer most of the stewardship contribution until they had income from the lot sales.

The restrictions on where not to develop (as identified by the sieve mapping design process) add value to those sites where development is appropriate. This makes the conservation development work. The challenge was figuring out the optimum level of restrictions. For example, unlike many developments, the house sites were not placed on the top of hills or ridges to maximize views. Instead, they hug the terrain for wind protection and to minimize their visual encroachment on the ranch. At the same time, they are positioned to take advantage of the

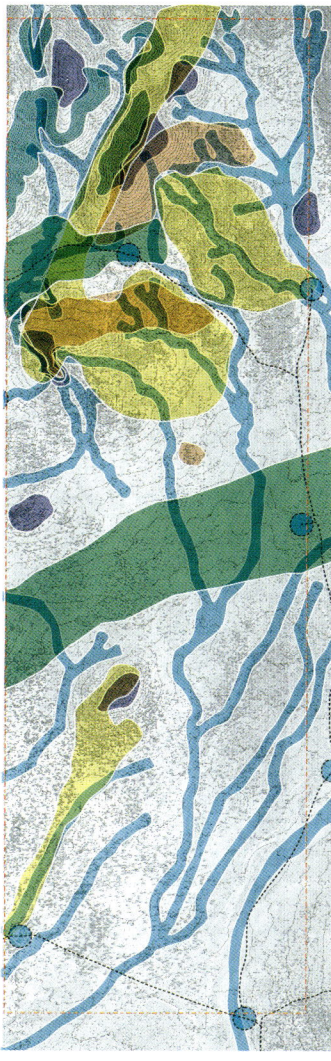
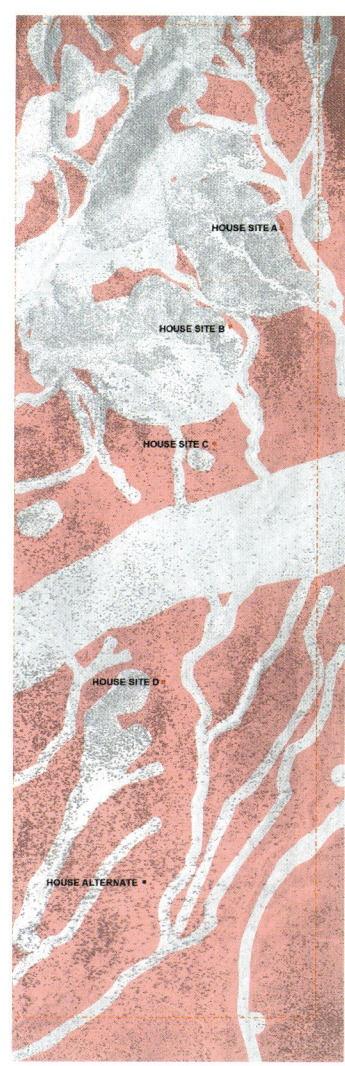
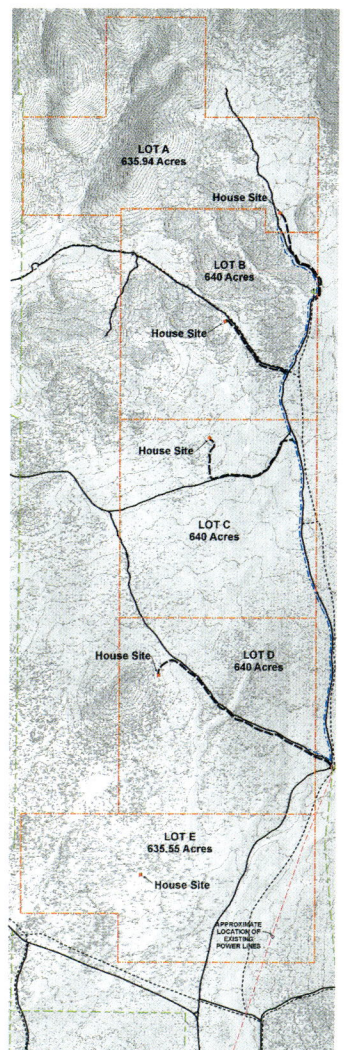

Figure 9.11 | Conservation Areas: This map creates a composite of all the preceding overlays shown in Figures 9.4–9.10. What this map reveals is a pattern of conservation priorities—an organic pattern based on what is considered to be important to protect. The land that falls through the "sieve" of the conservation priorities is the land that is appropriate for development. It is also the land whose value is most enhanced by the protection of what is not developed. The gray area on the composite map of the conservation areas becomes the red area on the following map of buildable land (Fig. 9.12).

Figure 9.12 | House Sites Relative to Buildable Land: This map corresponds to the land that has fallen through the "sieve" of conservation priorities (Fig. 9.11). The area of buildable land is mapped in red. The house sites are located within the area of buildable land; each site is a designated building envelope of 5,000 square feet. To further enhance the value of the property, each house site is located to be concealed from view of the other house sites.

Figure 9.13 | Lot Lines and Infrastructure: This map represents the lot lines relative to the house sites. It also shows the existing infrastructure and the improvements to the infrastructure that are required.

9.11   9.12   9.13

Case Studies   129

spectacular views of the nearby mountains. The restriction against building on hilltops or ridges adds value because it preserves the natural horizon for everyone's enjoyment, and protects the value of the land as a long-term investment. Land protection is the value-adding principle of the Montosa Ranch development.

In exchange for the restriction of being able to build a house within only a specified building envelope, the lot buyer gets the certainty of *never* having to look at the house of a neighbor. In exchange for the restriction against further subdivision, the lot buyer gets the certainty of a house site that is surrounded by land that will *never* be developed. What better way to protect the long-term value of one's investment? In exchange for the restriction against fencing the entire 640-acre lot, the lot buyer gets the right to ride a horse or hunt over a 32,000-acre ranch. In short, they get a ranch without having to worry about managing it. And they get to participate in land conservation in a meaningful way.

The Montosa Ranch Project is about capturing the conservation value of the land for the benefit of the ranch owners. It is also about promoting and financing land protection. When it is completed, the project will result in 27,000 acres of private land being protected from future development. It will also result in the ranch owners realizing their financial and estate planning goals without having to sell the ranch or destroy the integrity of the land. It is an important conservation project not only in terms of its size but also because it provides for the land's continued use as a cattle ranch. It establishes a powerful model that is consistent with B.W. Cox's goal of showing how the land can be managed for the future.

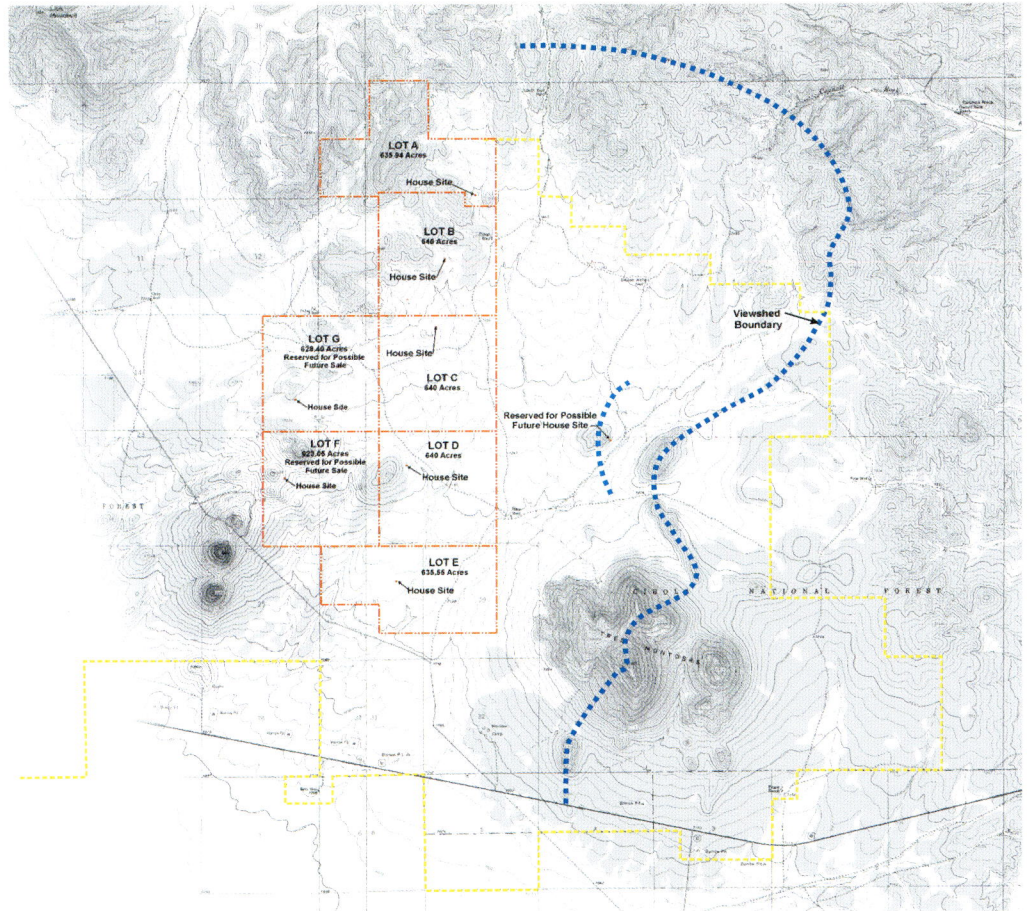

Figure 9.14 | House Sites Relative to Viewshed: This partial map of the ranch corresponds to the viewshed as defined by the topography. The viewshed describes what can be seen from the house sites. Because the house sites are located on east-facing slopes (for wind protection), the views from them are to the east. The dotted blue line, which runs along the top of the ridge to the east of the house sites, defines the viewshed.

In addition to protecting the viewshed, the house sites have been carefully located so that no house will be visible from any other house. This has been tested and proven by tethering helium balloons on 30 feet of rope at each house site. The house sites, therefore, can be marketed with the promise that the buyer will not see the house of a neighbor.

Figure 9.15 | **Analysis of House Site "A":** To prove the appropriateness of this house site, photographs were taken to document the relationship of the site to the landscape. In addition, an analytical diagram of each site relative to the features of the landscape was created.

opposite

Figure 9.16 | **Analysis of House Site "B":** To prove the appropriateness of this house site, photographs were taken to document the relationship of the site to the landscape. In addition, an analytical diagram of the site relative to the features of the landscape was created.

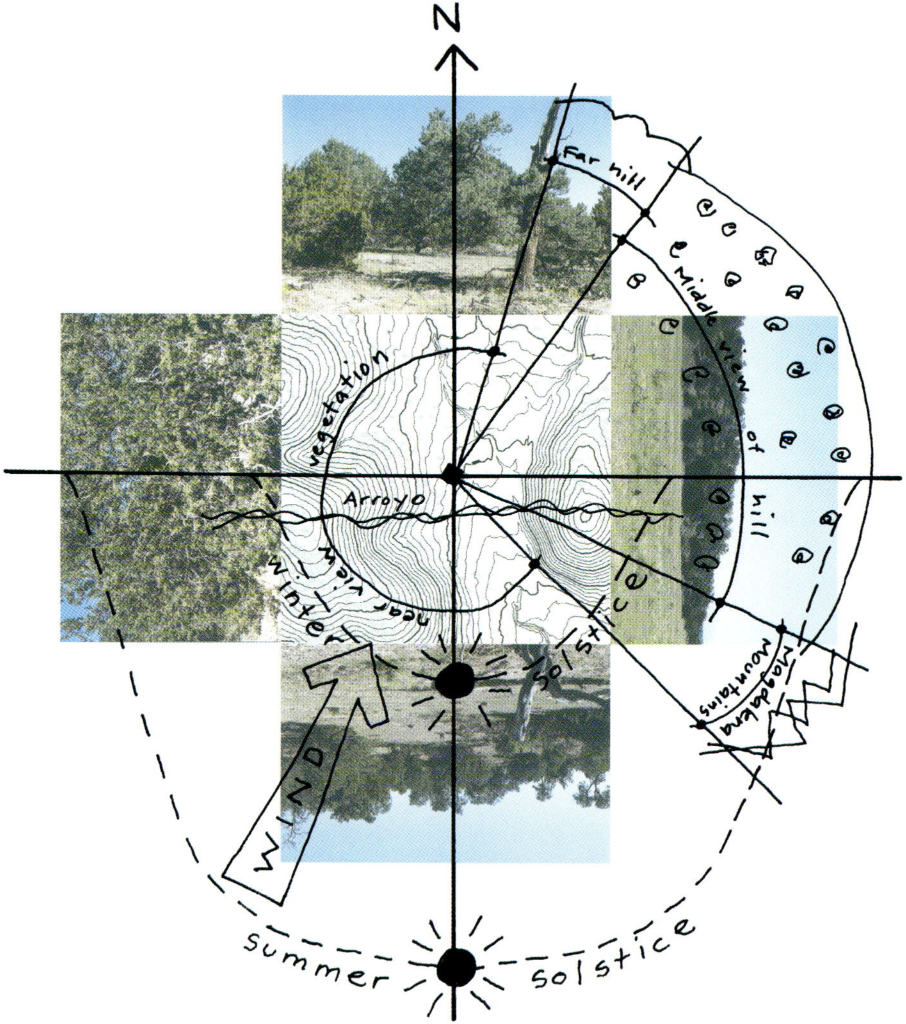

132 Saving the Ranch

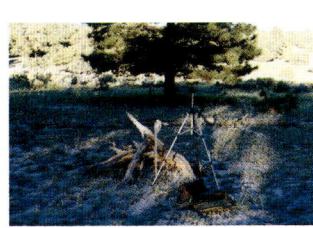

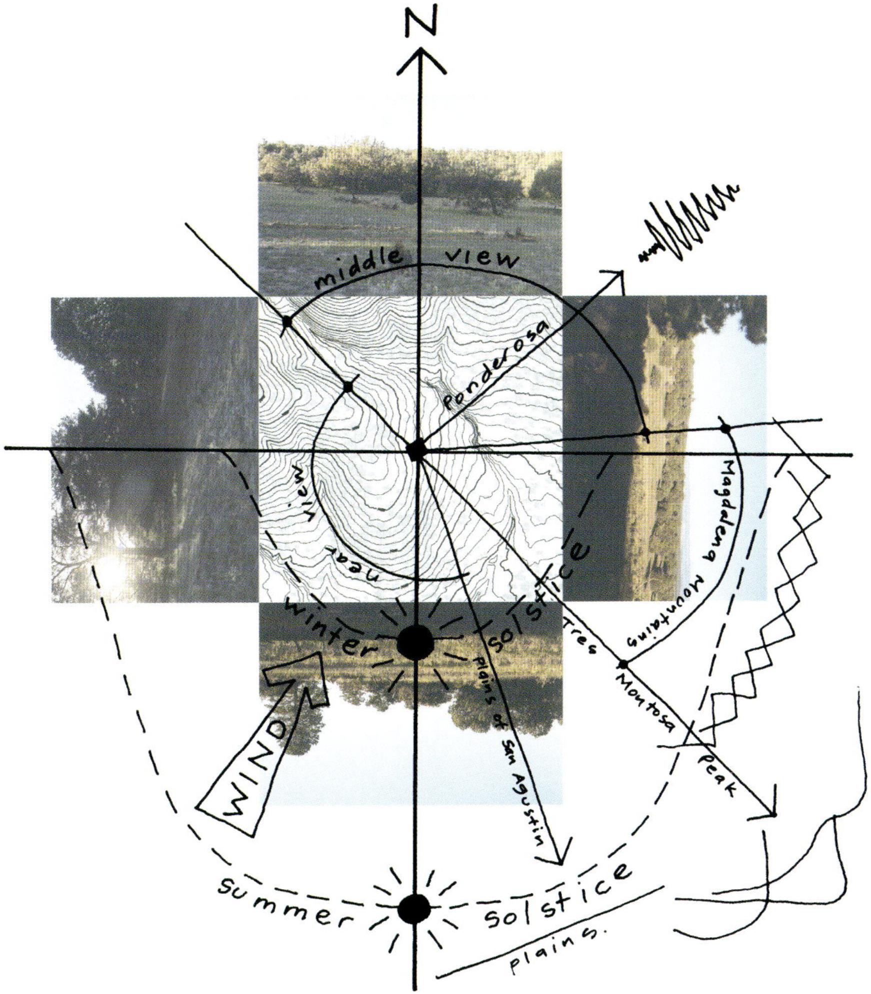
N
middle view
Ponderosa
near view
Magdalena Mountains
winter solstice
Tres Montosa Peak
plains of San Agustin
WIND
summer solstice
plains.

9.16

Figure 9.17 | **Analysis of House Site "C":** To prove the appropriateness of this house site, photographs were taken to document the relationship of the site to the landscape. In addition, an analytical diagram of the site relative to the features of the landscape was created.

opposite

Figure 9.18 | **Analysis of House Site "D":** To prove the appropriateness of this house site, photographs were taken to document the relationship of the site to the landscape. In addition, an analytical diagram of the site relative to the features of the landscape was created.

Figure 9.19 | **Analysis of House Site "E":** To prove the appropriateness of this house site, photographs were taken to document the relationship of the site to the landscape. In addition, an analytical diagram of the site relative to the features of the landscape was created.

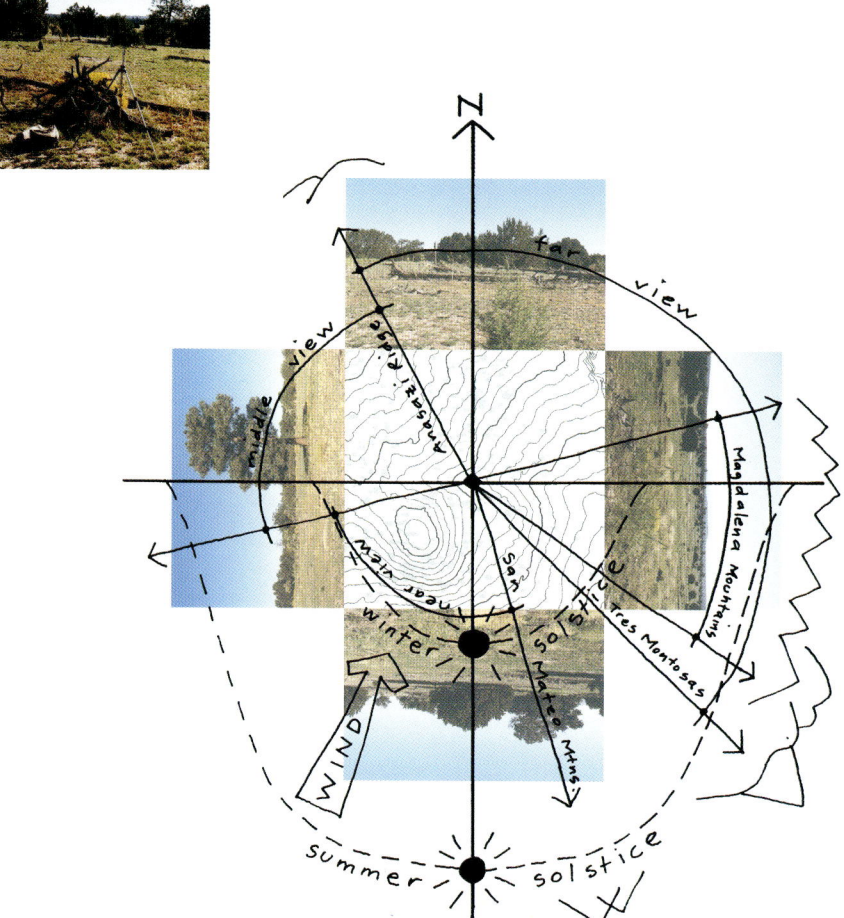

9.17

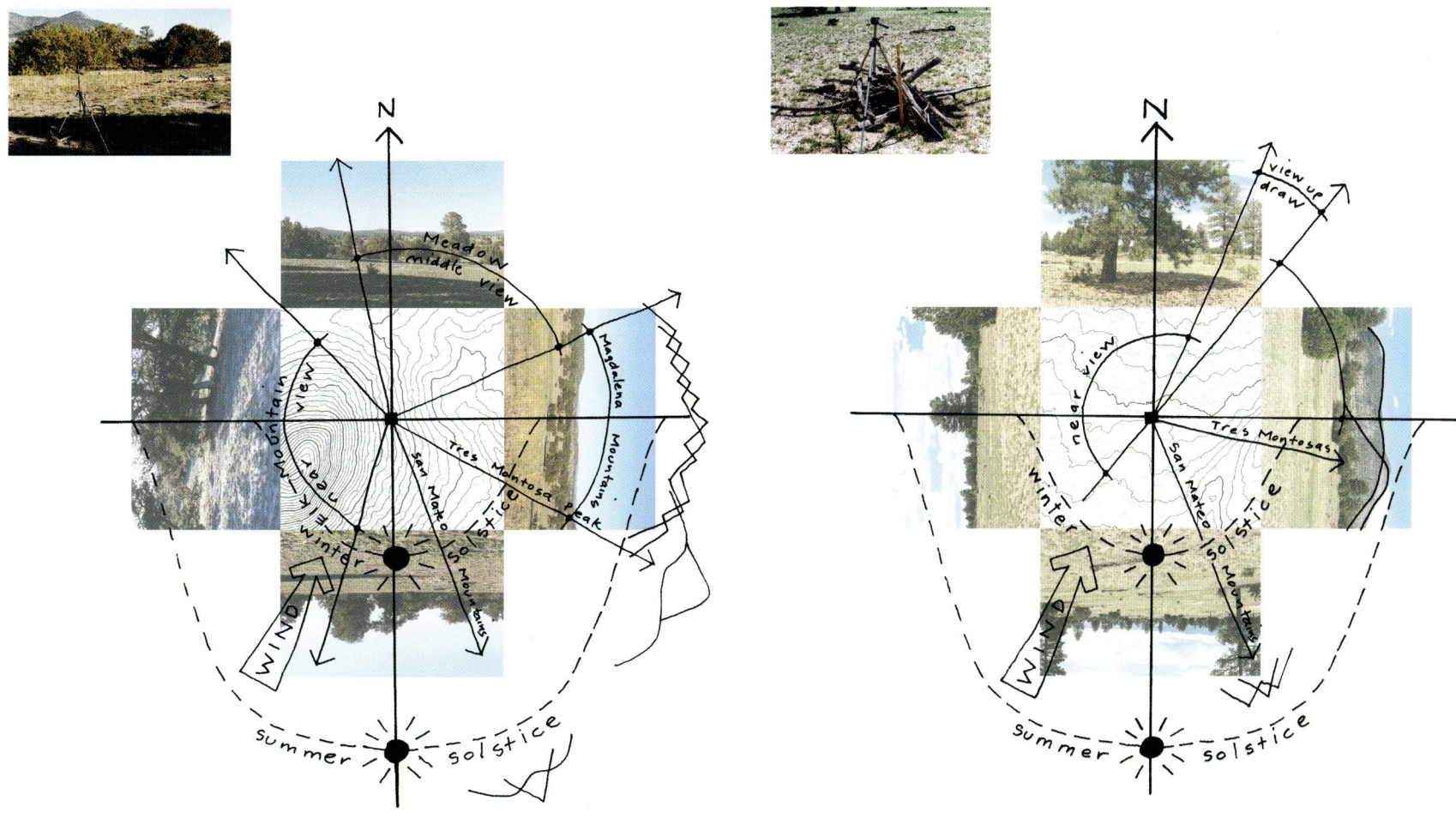

9.18

9.19

Case Studies 135

Repairing damage to buried water pipe caused by recent flash flood, Montosa Ranch.

Conservation easements depend on ranchers to be good stewards of the land. The role of the land trust is to enforce the legal restrictions on subdivision, development, mining, and other major land uses addressed in the conservation easement. The ideal is to have a working relationship based on mutual respect, with the land trust helping the landowner conserve the landscape they love.

Monitoring

Once a year, the land trust contacts the landowner to schedule a monitoring visit. This visit is required by law to keep the conservation easement in force. A land trust employee or board member visits the landowner to discuss any changes that have taken place on the property. The ranch is toured and pictures are taken at the photo points set up in the baseline report. An "Easement Monitoring Form" may be filled out. This could be a checklist or a set of written observations of the land's condition since the last visit. Major violations, such as a house built where it shouldn't have been built, are rare. If something is in doubt, the easement deed is reviewed ("Was that gravel pit there before?"). Clearly written easements present few problems. When too much detail or fuzzy restrictions are included, violations can occur as a result of confusion.

    A conservation easement should be written with a clear eye on the monitoring and enforcement responsibilities of the land trust. Easement restrictions should focus on fundamental land use practices where violations are visible, tangible, and genuinely damaging to significant conservation values. Simple easements work. Complex or poorly written easements interfere with ranching and cause problems. For example, restrictions on the stubble height of grass are not only unacceptable to most ranchers, they are also time-consuming and expensive to monitor. Transects of vegetation are similarly troublesome because variations in year-to-year rainfall can cause natural shifts in species abundance.

Migratory birds or elk may not be present during the monitoring visit but are at other times; the landowner will have sightings to report. In most cases, a continuation of historic ranch practices is all that is needed to support the habitat of threatened or endangered species. We must also accept the possibility of extirpation of a species through no fault of the rancher. However, if a rare plant population is wiped out because the rancher plowed an area that was off-limits, this is a clear violation.

Monitoring of open space values is more obvious. Does the ranch still provide open vistas? If the restrictions on subdivision and development are being honored, the answer is yes.

Trespassers sometimes plunder historic resources. The theft of potsherds, defacement of pictographs, removal of tipi rings, and other acts are usually not the fault of the landowner. The landowner is not held responsible for these acts of strangers who are out of the landowner's control.

Monitoring a conservation easement property should be done with common sense. The baseline report serves as the best source for understanding how a landscape works. Fires, floods, mudslides, avalanches, and droughts should be expected. Conservation easements are not intended to punish ranchers for natural events.

Enforcement

Of the 7,500 conservation easements in America, only 12 have had violations that needed to be resolved in court. Most of these have happened in the East where easements have been around for over a century and thousands of properties are involved. Typically, violations of easements tend to be resolved through a talk between the landowner and the land trust. If an easement has been properly written, a true violation occurs only when a landowner breaks their word and does something expressly prohibited.

Here are two typical cases of true violations:

In *Lunn v. the Tokekeke Association* (1992), Lunn bought a property under easement, then requested permission from the land trust to subdivide and develop it. The land trust rejected this request and Lunn sued. The Connecticut Supreme Court ruled in favor of the easement.

In *Sheftl v. Lebel* (1998), Lebel sued to violate an easement by building an elevated walkway and pier in a protected wetland. The Massachusetts Appeals Court ruled that a "plain language" reading of the easement meant the construction was not allowed.

The following two court cases offer different insights:

In *Burgess v. Breakell* (1995), Burgess tried to act as a third party by suing to have a conservation easement enforced to prohibit logging. The court ruled that Burgess held no legal standing. This case should reduce ranchers' concerns about third-party environmentalists suing to enforce easements.

The Whidbey-Camano Land Trust lost a case in Washington State where a landowner built a home outside of the prescribed building envelope. The judge ruled that the landowner acted in good faith because the envelope was not well identified. Well-written easements will not have this problem.

Legal cases reinforce the need to write clear easements. The courts rule based as much on "plain language" interpretations of the easement's purpose as on specific restrictions. This gives the best picture of the grantor's wishes. Attorneys may argue over the interpretation of one element of the document, but if the overall intent is spelled out clearly in the "whereas" clauses, the easement is likely to stand. Common law doctrines also played a role despite all the attention on specific federal and state statutes. Photo documentation is critical, and often is more relevant than highly technical text and scientific jargon. When a judge or jury can *see*

Historic ranch headquarters and formerly irrigated fields, Lake Valley Ranch.

an obvious violation, the case is easily made. Writing quality is critical as well. Easements based on model language fare much better than ones that deviate from proven formats.

The easement receiver or land trust must be willing and able to enforce the agreement. While most matters do not merit court action, true violations do. If the land trust exhausts all other attempts to resolve the violation by talking it over, it has a fiduciary responsibility to seek redress in court. This is a last resort and an expensive one. A lawsuit may cost both sides as much as $100,000 in legal fees and court costs. A typical easement deed outlines financial responsibilities related to court cases. If the land trust acts frivolously and no violation has occurred, they must pay the landowner's legal costs. If the land trust wins, the landowner pays the land trust's costs. The typical court-ordered remedy for construction of a prohibited house is to order it moved or torn down.

Legal action is used sparingly and only in extreme cases. A mutually trusted mediator can often resolve the dispute. Occasionally, an easement is amended to clear up a cloudy restriction. Sometimes an easement is amended to allow a violation that happened in good faith as a result of unclear wording, but only if the amendment clarifies the language to prevent similar misunderstandings in the future. A conservation easement can be amended only if the significant conservation values of the easement remain protected or if the protections are strengthened.

Trust

True stewardship comes from genuine caring for the land, not from a threat of punishment. Most easement donors possess a strong personal commitment to the land. They know its seasons, colors, moods, and limits. The deed is a legal recital of their love of a place, and violations are unlikely as long as the original grantor lives there. However, when a property is sold or transferred, the situation may change. The land trust can form a good working relationship with the new owner by offering help in explaining the easement and the landscape it protects. This is the moment when the wishes of the original grantor must be honored.

However, beyond all the legalities, conservation easements are about keeping our word and respecting the land. The lawyers are necessary only when we fail at both of these commitments.

Fenceline and cultivated fields, Lake Valley Ranch.

11 Saving the Ranch

As a livelihood, ranching represents a relationship between people and nature that is gradually being lost. Most people living today are removed from making their living on the land by four or five generations. For the majority of us, our food is grown thousands of miles away from where we live. We are isolated from the elements by the comforts of central air-conditioning. Our worldview is disconnected from any direct experience of being part of nature. As a result we lose sight of our interdependence with the earth, and forget how to sustain a balanced relationship with the land. Ranching serves as an important cultural link between the past and the future because someday we may need to remember how to work with nature, not against it.

To sustain life as a rancher requires taking care of the land. It requires respecting the delicate balance between rainfall and the land's capacity to support livestock without overgrazing. It also requires paying careful attention to which soils grow the best grass, where the winds come from, where the snow melts first, and where the most protected places are for calving. A rancher like B.W. Cox earns his livelihood based on his astute ability to read the land. Similarly, conservation easement design, to be successful, depends on the ability to read the land as well as on the ability to listen. Reading the land and listening to it have a lot in common: they both let the land do most of the talking.

Conservation easement design is important not only because it protects the open spaces that help remind us who we are as a people, but also because it provides for the continuation of a traditional way of living on the land. It promotes a relationship with the land that recognizes economic expedience while at the same time it affirms a land ethic that extends our notion of community to include all life: soils, waters, plants, animals, and human beings. If

> There are two spiritual dangers in not owning a farm. One is the danger of supposing that breakfast comes from the grocery, and the other that heat comes from the furnace.
> —Aldo Leopold

we don't share this commitment to where we live, then how can we promise our children the inheritance of a physical environment at least as good as we have inherited?

This book offers a way to honor this promise. There is more help out there in the agricultural organizations and land trusts of the West. Go to the Internet and type in www.lta.org—the Land Trust Alliance has a list of groups in every state. Call one of them and get to the bottom of this.

In the end, some ranchers will donate a conservation easement and some will not.

It's your land. You decide. But at least give the idea a chance.

Prepared by Tracy E. Conner, Esq., for the New Mexico Land Conservation Collaborative, and Clare C. Swanger, President of the New Mexico Land Conservation Collaborative.

This Deed of Conservation Easement ("Deed") is granted on this ___ day of _____, 200__, by _____, having an address at _____ (the "Landowner"), to the [name of land trust], a New Mexico nonprofit corporation, having an address at _____ (the "Land Trust"), for the purpose of forever conserving the natural and open space character and natural habitat of the subject property [*tailor as necessary to describe conservation values of property, including agricultural, recreational, historic, etc.*].

RECITALS

A. Property. The Landowner is the sole owner in fee simple of the property which is legally described in Exhibit 1 and shown in survey in Exhibit 2, attached to and made a part of this Deed (the "Property"), which consists of approximately _____ (___) acres of land, located in _____ County, State of New Mexico.

B. Water Rights. The Property has appurtenant water rights consisting of ___ acre feet of surface rights from the _____ [*name of acequia*] with a priority date of _____, ___, which are more particularly described in Exhibit 3 (the "Water Rights").

C. Mineral Rights. The Landowner owns all mineral rights with respect to the Property. All mineral rights associated with the Property and owned by the Landowner as of the date of this Deed are governed by the terms of this Deed.

OR

C. Mineral Rights. Certain mineral rights have been severed from the Property, but the possibility of future mining is so remote as to be negligible, as indicated by the geologist's report included with the baseline documentation report described below. All other mineral rights associated with the Property and owned by the Landowner as of the date of this Deed are governed by the terms of this Deed.

D. Scenic Values. The Property includes scenic open space consisting of _____ [*Describe location and views.*] The Property is visible from _____ [*Describe visibility from public roads and public lands and cite scenic designations, if any.*]

E. Biological Values. The Property contains significant relatively natural habitat and represents a high quality example of a [terrestrial-aquatic] ecosystem. _____ [*List flora and fauna, highlighting any that are threatened or endangered. Reference riparian areas. Reference adjacent natural areas. Reference biologist report, if any.*]

Appendix: Model Deed of Conservation Easement

F. <u>Agricultural Values</u>. The Property is primarily [prime farmland or farmland of statewide significance/ranchland] including _____ [*Describe property and length of time in agricultural production, if known. Cite USDA soil classifications, if any.*]

G. <u>Historical Values</u>. The Property contains _____ which is an historically important [land area/certified historic structure/archaeological site]. [*Cite listing on the National Register, or date of certification by Secretary of the Interior.*]

H. <u>Education and Recreation</u>. The Property possesses educational and/or recreational values which benefit the general public and consist of [trails, lake appropriate for boating, fishing stream, etc.].

I. <u>Governmental Policies</u>. The Property includes [open space/farmland/forestland], the preservation of which is pursuant to the following clearly delineated governmental policies:

[*Cite County and Municipal ordinances.*]

[*Sample state and federal legislation which may be cited if appropriate*]

(__)The New Mexico Land Use Easement Act, Sections 47-12-1 through 47-12-6 (NMSA 1978), which aids the landowner who wishes voluntarily to donate a conservation easement intended to restrict the use of a specific parcel of land so as to maintain in perpetuity the character of the land.

(__)The New Mexico Cultural Properties Preservation Easement Act, Sections 47-12A-1 through 47-12A-6 (NMSA 1978), which aids the landowner who wishes voluntarily to donate a conservation easement intended to restrict the use of a specific parcel of land so as to maintain in perpetuity the significant archaeological or historical character of that land.

(__)The New Mexico Right to Farm Act, Sections 47-9-1 through 47-9-4 (NMSA 1978), which declares the purpose "to conserve, protect, encourage, develop and improve agricultural land . . . and to reduce the loss to the state of its agricultural resources."

(__)The New Mexico Watershed District Act, Sections 73-20-3 through 73-20-49 (NMSA 1978), which states the Legislature's desire to further the "conservation . . . of water, and thereby preserve and protect New Mexico's land and water resources."

(__)The New Mexico Industrial and Agricultural Finance Authority Act, Sections 58-24-1 through 58-24-23 (NMSA 1978), which evidences the Legislature's concern for the maintenance of agriculturally productive resources, and its intention to encourage an increase in the inventory of agricultural lands and a resultant increase in the gainful employment of the citizens of the state.

(__)Property tax relief adopted by the State of New Mexico, which provides for tax relief for agricultural properties through a special method of valuation of land used primarily for agricultural purposes. Section 7-36-20 (NMSA 1978).

(__)The Federal Farmers Home Administration (FmHA) Instruction 1951-S (7 C.F.R. 1951 Subpart S), which states a public policy to "keep the farmer on the farm."

(__)The Federal Farmland Protection Policy Act, 7 U.S.C. Sections 4201 through 4209, which committed the federal government to the goal of conserving farmland in carrying out its public works and other development projects.

J. <u>Public Benefit</u>. Conserving the scenic, biological, agricultural, historical, educational, and recreational values described above (collectively, the "Conservation Purposes") of the Property is consistent with, and important to, the history, culture, and economy of the area, which is under increasing threat of development and fragmentation, and will result in a significant public benefit to the people of _____ County, the people of the State of New Mexico, and the people of this nation.

[*May also add some or all of the following, and adjust depending upon the specific attributes of the property subject to the easement:*]

It is a significant public benefit for this Property to be preserved, because:

(__)The Property possesses significant natural, agricultural, ecological, scenic, wildlife, habitat, and open space values of great importance to Landowner, to Land Trust, to _____ County, to the State of New Mexico, and to the people of this nation;

(__)Agriculture has been an integral part of the way of life in _____ County for centuries and should be preserved in order to protect the area's great natural beauty, scenic vistas, and way of life;

(__)Open space has been an integral part of _____ County for centuries and should be preserved in order to protect the area's great natural beauty and scenic vistas;

(__)The Property exists in an area where development is occurring and is expected to occur at an accelerated rate in the future;

(__)The Property includes an acequia, long important to the irrigated farmland, agricultural productivity, traditional way of life and culture of the _____ area and northern New Mexico;

(__)The use of the Property as stated in this Deed is intended to be consistent with public programs for conservation in the area, including programs for irrigation, soil protection, and agricultural uses;

(__)The development of the Property would impair the scenic character of the local rural landscape and would contribute to the degradation of the natural character, agricultural productivity, riparian ecology, and wildlife habitat of the area;

(__)The Property has been evaluated for scenic quality using the [Name of Land Trust]'s Review Process for Scenic Attributes, a rigorous review process for scenic attributes, and found to be scenic, and easily seen by the public;

(__)The Property is in a relatively natural state, and includes important natural habitat for _____ [*beaver, muskrat, herons, owls, eagles, ducks, geese, hawks, coyote, fox, deer, elk, other waterfowl, birds, fish, trees, flowers, other plants, etc.*];

Model Deed of Conservation Easement 149

(__)Portions of the Property contain _____ [*petroglyphs, etc.*] of an archaeological and historic nature.

K. <u>Baseline Documentation Report</u>. The characteristics of the Property and its current use and state of improvement are described in a Baseline Documentation Report prepared by the Landowner with the cooperation of the Land Trust. The Baseline Documentation Report has been acknowledged by the Landowner and the Land Trust to be complete and accurate as of the date of this Deed. Both the Landowner and the Land Trust have copies of this report, and a copy will be retained in the Land Trust's files.

L. <u>Qualifications</u>. The Land Trust is a nonprofit, tax-exempt organization qualified under Sections 501(c)(3) and 170(b)(1)(A)(vi) of the Internal Revenue Code (the "Code"), a "qualified organization" as defined by Section 170(h)(3) of the Code, and a qualified "holder" as defined by Section 47-12-2A of the Land Use Easement Act.

M. <u>Intent</u>. The Landowner intends to make a charitable gift to the Land Trust of the property interest conveyed by this Deed for the purpose of assuring that, under the Land Trust's perpetual stewardship, the Conservation Purposes will be maintained forever and uses of the Property that are inconsistent with the Conservation Purposes will be prevented or corrected.

AGREEMENT

NOW, THEREFORE, in consideration of the mutual promises and covenants contained herein, the Landowner conveys to the Land Trust a "land use easement" as defined by Section 47-12-2B of the Land Use Easement Act (the "Easement"), which is also a "qualified real property interest" as defined by Section 170(h)(2)(C) of the Code, the conveyance of which is the gift of a "qualified conservation contribution" as defined by Section 170(h) of the Code.

I. <u>Prohibited Acts</u>. The Landowner shall not perform, nor knowingly allow others to perform, any act on or affecting the Property that is inconsistent with the Conservation Purposes enumerated in this Deed. The Landowner and the Land Trust acknowledge, however, that the uses of the Property and the improvements to the Property described in this Deed and in the Baseline Documentation Report are consistent with the Conservation Purposes. However, unless otherwise specified below, nothing in this Deed shall require the Landowner to take any action to restore the condition of the Property after any Act of God or other event over which they had no control. The Landowner understands that nothing in this Deed relieves them of any obligation or restriction on the use of the Property imposed by law.

A. <u>Construction</u>. The construction of any temporary or permanent buildings, facilities, or structures of any kind is prohibited except: _____. [*Tailor to specific situation. Can include language about permitted agricultural structures, fences, homesites, lighting, size and height limitations, mobile homes/temporary structures, etc.*] Prior to undertaking any construction permitted herein, and prior to applying for a building permit for such construction, the Landowner shall notify the Land Trust in writing and provide the Land Trust with the opportunity to review the plans for such construction for compliance with the terms of this Deed.

B. <u>Subdivision</u>. The division or subdivision of the Property into two or more parcels, whether by physical or legal process, is prohibited. Creation of a condominium or any *de facto* division of the Property is prohibited. Lot line adjustments or lot consolidation without the prior written consent of the Land Trust is prohibited. The Property [can/cannot] be used to meet zoning calculations for building or development outside the Property, [eliminate following phrase OR tailor to specific situation] except for the addition of _____ within the [building envelope] as shown on the Survey. The Landowner may transfer undivided interests in the Property, provided, however, that no cotenant or owner of an undivided interest shall have the right, either independently or through legal action, to have the property physically or legally partitioned. The Landowner shall notify the Land Trust immediately of the name and address of any grantee of an undivided interest in the Property.

C. <u>Water Rights</u>. Except as specifically provided below, the voluntary separation of Water Rights from the Property is prohibited. The Landowner shall take all prudent measures, including timely payment of assessments, beneficial use of water, and participation in conservation programs, to avoid forfeiture or abandonment of the Water Rights. Should the Landowner be notified for any reason regarding possible forfeiture or abandonment of any of the Water Rights, the Landowner shall immediately notify the Land Trust in writing and arrange for the beneficial use of the Water Rights on the Property. If for any reason the Landowner is unable to beneficially use the Water Rights on the Property, the Landowner shall (i) transfer the Water Rights to the Land Trust or to a third party designated by the Land Trust; (ii) with the express written consent of the Land Trust, lease the Water Rights to a third party; or (iii) with the express written consent of the Land Trust, place the Water Rights in a Land Trust approved conservation program that meets applicable criteria.

D. <u>Agriculture</u>. All farming, ranching, and agricultural practices shall be conducted in a sustainable manner, and in keeping with practices that are best suited for the conservation of soil and water, the maintenance of soil and water quality, and so as to avoid erosion, overgrazing, soil contamination, and water pollution. The establishment of any feedlot (defined as a permanently constructed confined area or facility within which the land is not grazed or cropped annually, and which is used for the reception, feeding and/or slaughter of animals) on the Property is prohibited. The Landowner and the Land Trust desire to encourage the continuation of agricultural activities on the Property and to provide sufficient flexibility so that the Landowner can take advantage of appropriate practices and technologies in the future, all in a manner consistent with and in furtherance of the Conservation Purposes.

E. <u>Timber</u>. Commercial harvesting of timber or wood products on the Property is prohibited. Timber or wood products may be removed only to prevent encroachment onto open fields, to control insects or disease, to thin stands appropriately for fire management, to prevent personal injury and property damage, to provide firewood for use on the Property, and to cut posts for maintaining and constructing fences on the Property. [*If Landowner wants to retain the right for future use of the Property as a tree farm, or for limited, sustainable timbering, add language relevant to those activities and a statement that these activities may not compromise the Conservation Purposes. Working forest easements or easements which contemplate substantial timber harvesting require additional language and often include the preparation of a forest management plan along with notice to or approval by the Land Trust.*]

F. <u>Utilities</u>. Aboveground utilities (including electric, sewer, water, telephone, cable, gas, etc.), except for those currently located on the Property or specifically anticipated by the Landowner and described in the Baseline Documentation Report, are prohibited. Prior to placing any utilities underground, the Landowner shall notify the Land Trust in writing, specifying the type and location of such utilities and the steps to be taken to protect the Conservation Purposes.

G. <u>Roads</u>. The construction of roads is prohibited except: _____ _____.

[*Tailor to specific situation; specify surface requirements and prohibitions if desired*.] Prior to undertaking any of the construction of any roads permitted herein, and prior to applying for any permits necessary for such construction, the Landowner shall notify the Land Trust in writing and provide the Land Trust with the opportunity to review the plans for such construction for compliance with the terms of this Deed.

H. <u>Impervious Surfaces</u>. Paving, covering, or treating the soil with an impervious surface, including concrete, asphalt, or any other material, is prohibited except for roads specifically permitted by this Deed or as foundations for construction specifically permitted by this Deed. Any use of the Property which causes any of its surfaces, other than roads permitted pursuant to subparagraph G above, to become relatively impervious or eroded (through either compaction, denuding the land, or otherwise) is prohibited.

I. <u>Mining</u>. Soil, sand, gravel, and rock may be extracted from the Property provided that such extraction is solely for use on the Property, that not more than one acre of the Property is disturbed by such extraction, and that such extraction is done in a manner consistent with the Conservation Purposes and is consistent with Section 170(h) of the Code and the Treasury Regulations adopted pursuant thereto. Any other mining or extraction, or consent by the Landowner to any mining or extraction, of soil, sand, gravel, rock, hydrocarbons, or any mineral substance, using a surface mining method or any other extractive technique that is inconsistent with the Conservation Purposes, is prohibited. Consent to any mining or surface mining on the Property under the New Mexico Surface Mining Act, Sections 69-25A-1 through 69-25A-35 (NMSA 1978) or its successor statute, or any other New Mexico surface mining consent law, is prohibited. In addition, no mining shall be conducted within _____ (____) feet of_____.
[*Specify any distances such activity must be from wetland or other sensitive areas.*]

J. <u>Refuse</u>. The dumping, accumulation, or storage of any kind of refuse on the Property is prohibited. Should refuse be found on the Property, it is the Landowner's responsibility to remove it. This section ("Refuse") shall not, however, prevent the storage of agricultural supplies, agricultural equipment, and agricultural products on the Property, so long as such storage is done in a manner consistent with the Conservation Purposes.

K. <u>Commercial Activity</u>.

(a) *Generally*. Commercial or industrial activity related to the producing, buying, or selling of goods or services, other than home occupations or recreational activity (both described below), and commercial activity related to agricultural products grown on the Property and agricultural services performed on the Property, are prohibited.

(b) *Home Occupations.* Nothing in this section ("Commercial Activity") shall prohibit the conduct of "home occupations" permitted by applicable zoning codes, if any, which home occupations are carried out exclusively within structures permitted by the terms of this Deed, and which home occupations are consistent with the Conservation Purposes.

(c) *Recreation.* More than a *de minimis* use of the Property for commercial recreational activity is prohibited, provided, however, that if low impact, seasonal, commercial hunting is determined by a court of competent jurisdiction to be more than a *de minimis* use, then this subparagraph ("Recreation") shall be of no force or effect. All-terrain vehicles and snowmobiles are not permitted on the Property except as may be necessary in connection with agricultural use of the Property pursuant to subparagraph D above.

L. Signs. Signs are permitted for purposes of identifying the Property as private property, posting the Property against trespassing or hunting, identifying the Property as protected by the Land Trust, or any posting or notice required by law. All other signs are prohibited. Signs shall not exceed one (1) by two (2) feet in size, be made with reflective surfaces, or be artificially illuminated.

M. Public Access. This Deed is not intended to provide for public access to the Property. The Landowner retains the right to allow public access to the Property in the future provided that such public access complies with the terms of this Deed and is consistent with and not to the detriment of the Conservation Purposes. The Land Trust shall have no obligation to take any action to prevent trespassing on the Property. [*Easements that are exclusively for historic preservation require some public access.*]

2. Rights Retained by Landowner. Landowner reserves to himself/herself and to his/her personal representatives, heirs, successors, and assigns, all rights not expressly prohibited or limited by this easement, including all rights accruing from his/her ownership of the Property, the right to engage in or permit or invite others to engage in all uses of the Property that are not expressly prohibited herein and are not inconsistent with the purpose of this easement, the right to exclude any member of the public from trespassing on the Property, the right to sell or otherwise transfer the Property to anyone they chose, and the right to mortgage the Property, so long as the mortgage is subordinated to this Deed.

3. Perpetual Duration. The Easement shall run with the land in perpetuity. Every provision of this Deed that applies to the Landowner or Land Trust shall also apply to their respective heirs, executors, administrators, assigns, and all other successors in interest as their interests may appear. A party's rights and obligations under this Deed terminate upon transfer of the party's interest in this Deed or the Property except that liability for acts or omissions prior to transfer shall survive transfer.

4. Responsibilities of Landowner. Other than as specified herein, this Deed is not intended to impose any legal or other responsibili-

ty on the Land Trust, or in any way to affect any obligation of the Landowner as owner of the Property, including:

(a) *Taxes*. The Landowner is solely responsible for payment of all taxes and assessments levied against the Property. If the Land Trust is ever required to pay any taxes or assessments on its interest in the Property, the Landowner shall reimburse the Land Trust for the same, and until such reimbursement occurs, such payment shall constitute a lien on the Property.

(b) *Upkeep and Maintenance*. The Landowner is solely responsible for the upkeep and maintenance of the Property.

(c) *Liability and Indemnification*. The Landowner is solely responsible for liability arising from or related to the Property, including injury (bodily or otherwise) or damage to any person or organization directly or indirectly caused by any action or omission of the Landowner. If the Land Trust is ever required by a court to pay damages resulting from personal injury, property damage, loss, or theft that occurs on the Property, the Landowner shall indemnify and reimburse the Land Trust for these payments, as well as for the Land Trust's costs and reasonable attorneys' fees and other expenses of defending itself, unless the Land Trust or any of its agents have committed a deliberate act that is determined by a court to be the proximate cause of the injury or damage.

(d) *Insurance*. Landowner warrants that the Land Trust is and will continue to be an additional insured on Landowner's liability insurance policy covering the Property. Landowner shall provide certificates of such insurance to Land Trust within thirty (30) days after the date of recordation of this Deed and subsequently, upon Land Trust's written request therefor. Landowner shall advise Land Trust at least thirty (30) days in advance of cancellation of any insurance policy.

5. <u>Landowner Warranties</u>.

(a) *Title Warranty*. The Landowner warrants that the Landowner has good and sufficient title to the Property, and that there are no liens on, leases to, or other interests in the Property that have not been disclosed to the Land Trust in writing. The Landowner hereby promises to defend the Property and the Easement against all claims from persons claiming by, through, or under the Landowner.

[*OR, if there is a mortgage on the property:*]

(a) *Title Warranty*. The Landowner warrants that the Landowner has good and sufficient title to the Property, that the lien on the Property held by_____ dated _____, has been subordinated to this Deed as shown in Exhibit 4, and that there are no other liens on, leases to, or other interests in the Property that have not been disclosed to the Land Trust in writing. The Landowner hereby promises to defend the Property and the Easement against all claims from persons claiming by, through, or under the Landowner.

(b) *Environmental Warranty*. The Landowner warrants that the Landowner has no knowledge of a release or threatened release of hazardous substances on the Property. The Landowner shall indemnify, defend, and hold harmless the Land Trust against all litigation, claims, demands, penalties, damages, losses, and expenses of any kind, including reasonable attorneys' fees, arising from or connected with any release of hazardous substances or violation of federal, state, or local laws. Nothing in this Deed shall be construed as giving rise to any right or ability in the Land Trust, nor shall the Land Trust have any right or ability, to exercise physical or managerial control over the day-to-day operations of the Property, or otherwise to become an operator with respect to the Property within the meaning of the Comprehensive Environmental Response, Compensation and Liability Act of 1980, as amended, or successor statutes.

6. <u>Inspection</u>.

(a) *Annual*. With reasonable advance notice to the Landowner, representatives of the Land Trust may enter the Property at reasonable times for the purpose of inspecting the Property to determine if there is compliance with the terms of this Deed. Inspections will generally occur once a year but may occur whenever the Land Trust deems appropriate.

(b) *Emergency*. If the Land Trust believes or had reason to believe that there is an ongoing, imminent, or threatened violation of the terms of this Deed, the Land Trust may enter the Property for the purpose of inspecting the Property to determine if there is compliance with the terms of this Deed. The Land Trust will use good faith efforts to contact the Landowner, but the Land Trust may enter the Property without the Landowner's presence.

7. <u>Enforcement</u>. The Land Trust has all the rights, remedies, and powers to enforce the terms of this Deed against the Landowner that are provided by law. Except when an ongoing or imminent violation could irreversibly diminish or impair the Conservation Purposes, the Land Trust shall give the Landowner written notice of the violation and thirty (30) days to correct it before filing any legal action. If a court with jurisdiction determines that a violation may exist or has occurred, the Land Trust may obtain an injunction to stop the violation, temporarily or permanently, and to restore the Property to its condition prior to the violation. In any case where a court finds that a violation has occurred, the Landowner shall reimburse the Land Trust for all its expenses incurred in stopping and correcting the violation, including reasonable attorneys' fees and court costs. If the court finds no violation, the Landowner and Land Trust shall each bear their own expenses and attorneys' fees. The Landowner and the Land Trust agree that this allocation of expenses is appropriate in light of the potential disparate financial incentives of the Landowner and the Land Trust and the Land Trust's public benefit mission.

8. <u>Transfer of Easement</u>. The Easement, and the rights and responsibilities contained in this Deed, may be transferred by the Land Trust to another organization only pursuant to the subsections below:

(a) *Involuntary*. If the Land Trust ever ceases to exist or no longer qualifies under Section 170(h)(3) of the Internal Revenue Code or applicable state law, a court with jurisdiction shall transfer the Easement to another organization having similar purposes, that is qualified under Section 170(h)(3) of the Internal Revenue Code and applicable state law, and that agrees to monitor the Easement and enforce the terms of this Deed.

(b) *Voluntary*. If the Land Trust ever wishes voluntarily to transfer the Easement, the Land Trust will notify the Landowner in writing and give the Landowner sixty (60) days from receipt of notification in which to deliver any preferences the Landowner may have regarding a successor organization. The Easement shall only be transferred to another organization having similar purposes, that is qualified under Section 170(h)(3) of the Internal Revenue Code and applicable state law, and that agrees to monitor the Easement and enforce the terms of this Deed.

9. Amendment. The Landowner and the Land Trust recognize that circumstances could arise which might justify the modification of certain provisions of this Deed. The Landowner and the Land Trust have the right to agree to amendments to this Deed provided that, in the reasonable discretion of the Land Trust, such amendment enhances the Conservation Purposes. In no event, however, shall any amendment be made that: (i) adversely affects the qualification of the Easement under any applicable laws, including Section 170(h) of the Internal Revenue Code; (ii) adversely affects the status of the Land Trust under any applicable laws, including Section 501(c)(3) of the Internal Revenue Code; or (iii) affects the perpetual duration of this Deed. This Deed shall not be altered, changed, or amended other than by a written instrument executed by the parties and recorded in the Office of the County Clerk of the county in which this Deed was recorded. Nothing in this section ("Amendment") shall require the Landowner or the Land Trust to agree to, or negotiate regarding, any proposed amendment.

10. Termination.

(a) *Condemnation*. If all or a part of the Property is taken for public use (or sold to a public authority under threat of condemnation), and the Easement is terminated in whole or in part, then the Land Trust shall be entitled to a percentage of the condemnation award or sale proceeds (net of any increase in value attributable to improvements made after the date of this Deed) equal to the ratio, as of the date of this Deed, of the appraised value of the Easement to the unrestricted fair market value of the Property.

(b) *Changed Conditions*. The Landowner and the Land Trust recognize that conditions on or surrounding the Property could change so much in the future that it becomes impossible to protect and preserve the Conservation Purposes. The Landowner and the Land Trust have the right to jointly request that a court with jurisdiction terminate all or a portion of the Easement created by this Deed and order the sale of the Property. Upon such termination of the Easement and sale of the Property, the Land Trust shall be entitled to a percentage of the sale proceeds (net of any increase in value attributable to improvements made after the date of this Deed) equal to the ratio, as of the date of this Deed, of the appraised value of the Easement to the unrestricted fair market value of the Property.

[*If the Landowner is not taking a tax deduction for the donation of the Easement, a specific percentage should be substituted for the ratio described in subsections (a) and (b) above.*]

(c) *Other Termination Provisions*. The Easement conveyed by this Deed constitutes a property right, immediately vested in the Land

Trust, which the parties stipulate to have a fair market value determined as set forth above. Nothing in this section ("Termination") shall require the Landowner or the Land Trust to agree to, or negotiate regarding, any proposed termination. Any funds received by the Land Trust pursuant to this section ("Termination") shall be used by the Land Trust in a manner consistent with the Conservation Purposes exemplified by this Deed.

11. <u>Approvals</u>. Before doing anything that requires the Land Trust's consent or approval pursuant to this Deed, the Landowner shall seek such approval from the Land Trust in writing. Any consent or approval by the Land Trust permitted or required by this Deed for uses or acts that are conditional or not expressly reserved by the Landowner may be granted only if the Land Trust has determined in its reasonable discretion, that the proposed use or act conforms to the intent of this Deed, meets any applicable conditions stated herein, and is consistent with and not to the detriment of the Conservation Purposes. The Land Trust shall grant or withhold its consent or approval in writing within forty-five (45) days of receipt of the Landowner's written request therefor, and failure of the Land Trust to respond within such time period shall be deemed the Land Trust's consent or approval.

12. <u>Notices</u>.

(a) *Generally*. Prior to exercising any right reserved under this Deed which may have an adverse impact on the Conservation Purposes the Landowner will notify the Land Trust. Any notices permitted or required by this Deed shall be in writing and shall be personally delivered or sent by certified mail, return receipt requested.

(b) *Current Addresses*. As of the date of this Deed, the addresses for the Landowner and the Land Trust are as follows:
To the Landowner: _____
_____
_____

To the Land Trust: _____
_____
_____

(c) *Permanent Addresses*. In addition to the foregoing, the address of the Property, as stated in the recitals, shall always be a valid address for notices to the Landowner, and the address of the Land Trust's registered agent, on file with the State of New Mexico, shall always be a valid address for notices to the Land Trust.

13. <u>Compliance Certificates</u>. Within thirty (30) days following receipt of written request from the Landowner, the Land Trust shall execute a compliance certificate and deliver it to the Landowner to certify to the best of the Land Trust's knowledge the Landowner's compliance (or noncompliance) with any obligation of the Landowner contained in this Deed.

14. <u>Subsequent Mortgages</u>. No provision of this Deed should be construed as impairing the ability of the Landowner to use the Property as collateral for subsequent borrowing, provided that any mortgage or lien arising from such a borrowing shall be subordinated to this Deed.

15. <u>Waiver</u>. No term of this Deed shall be deemed waived unless

such waiver is in writing signed by the party making the waiver. No forbearance, delay, or failure to exercise any right, power, or remedy shall impair such right, power, or remedy, shall be construed as a waiver of such right, power, or remedy, or shall prevent the exercising of such right, power, or remedy in the future.

16. Incorporation. The recitals set forth at the beginning of this Deed, and any exhibits referenced herein and attached hereto, are incorporated herein by this reference.

17. Interpretation. This Deed was negotiated and entered into in the State of New Mexico and shall be governed by the laws of the State of New Mexico. This Deed shall not be interpreted for or against any party on the basis of authorship, but rather shall be interpreted so as to give maximum protection to the Conservation Purposes. The captions and section headings of this Deed are not intended or represented to be descriptive of all the terms thereunder, and such captions and section headings shall not be deemed to limit, define, or enlarge the terms of this Deed. The use of the words "include" and "including" shall be construed as if the phrases "without limitation" or "but not [be] limited to" were annexed thereafter.

18. Severability. If any provision of this Deed or the application thereof to any person or circumstance is found to be illegal, invalid, or unenforceable, the remainder of the provisions of this Deed shall not be affected thereby.

19. Integration. This Deed sets forth the entire agreement of the parties with respect to the Easement and supersedes all prior discussions, negotiations, understandings, documents, or agreements relating to this Deed or the Easement.

20. Acceptance. Pursuant to the Resolution by the Board of Directors of the Land Trust adopted on _____, 200__, attached hereto as Exhibit 5, the Land Trust has accepted the Easement conveyed by this Deed and the rights and responsibilities described in this Deed.

To Have and To Hold, this Deed of Conservation Easement unto the Land Trust, its successors and assigns, forever.

In Witness Whereof, the Landowner and the Land Trust, intending to legally bind themselves, have set their hands on the date first written above.

"Landowner"
_____
[Name]

"Land Trust"
[Name of Land Trust],
a New Mexico nonprofit corporation

By:_____
Name:_____
Title:_____

ACKNOWLEDGMENTS

County of _____)
) ss
State of _____)

The foregoing instrument was acknowledged before me this ____ day of _____, 200__, by _____.

_____
Notary Public (SEAL)

My commission expires: _____

County of _____)
) ss
State of _____)

The foregoing instrument was acknowledged before me this ____ day of _____, 200___, by _____, the _____ [title] of _____ [name of land trust].

_____
Notary Public (SEAL)

My commission expires: _____

Exhibit 1 to Deed of Conservation Easement

LEGAL DESCRIPTION

[*To be added.*]

Exhibit 2 to Deed of Conservation Easement

SURVEY OF PROPERTY

[*To be added.*]

Exhibit 3 to Deed of Conservation Easement

WATER RIGHTS

[*To be added.*]

Exhibit 4 to Deed of Conservation Easement

MORTGAGE SUBORDINATION AGREEMENT

For good and valuable consideration, the receipt and sufficiency of which are hereby acknowledged, the undersigned _____, a _____, as Mortgagee of that certain Real Estate Mortgage recorded _____ ____, 19___ in Book _____ at page _____ in the records of the _____ County Clerk, _____ County, New Mexico, hereby consent to the execution of that certain Deed of Conservation Easement by _____, as Landowners, to the [Name of Land Trust], a New Mexico nonprofit organization, as Land Trust, subordinate the lien of the Real Estate Mortgage to the Deed of Conservation Easement, and agree that any foreclosure of the Real Estate Mortgage shall not adversely affect the existence or continuing validity of the Deed of Conservation Easement, which Deed of Conservation Easement shall run with the land and remain in full force and effect as if such Deed of Conservation Easement were executed, delivered, and recorded prior to the execution, delivery, and recording of the Real Estate Mortgage. This subordination of _____ mortgage shall pertain only to the property described in the attached exhibit.

IN WITNESS WHEREOF, the undersigned has executed this Subordination as of _____ ____, 200___.

[Name of Mortgagee]

By:_____
Name:_____
Title:_____
[*Add acknowledgment block for representative of mortgagee.*]

Exhibit 5 to Deed of Conservation Easement

RESOLUTION BY THE BOARD OF DIRECTORS OF
[*Name of land trust*]
REGARDING THE _____ CONSERVATION EASEMENT

The following Resolution was passed by the Board of Directors of the [Name of Land Trust] on _____ ____, 200__, as recorded in the Minutes of the Board Meeting:

"RESOLVED by the Board of Directors of the [Name of Land Trust] that a Deed of Conservation Easement from _____ to the [Name of Land Trust] conserving certain conservation purposes on _____ (____) acres of [irrigated farmland/scenic open space/wildlife habitat/educational or recreational land/historic property] be accepted by the [Name of Land Trust], that the [Name of Land Trust] accepts all of the rights and responsibilities described in said Deed, and that the Secretary of the Board of Directors of the [Name of Land Trust], _____, is hereby authorized by the Board of Directors to act on its behalf to finalize and execute said Deed on behalf of the [Name of Land Trust]."

By:_____ Date:_____
_____, Secretary

Looking south to San Mateo Mountains and the Plains of San Agustín, Montosa Ranch.

Bibliography

Arendt, Randall G. *Conservation Design for Subdivisions: A Practical Guide to Creating Open Space Networks*. Washington, DC: Island Press, 1996.

Bick, Steven and Harry L. Haney, Jr. *The Landowner's Guide to Conservation Easements*. Dubuque, Iowa: Kendall/Hunt Publishing Company, 2001.

Cosgrove, Jeremiah P. and Julia Freedgood. *Your Land Is Your Legacy: A Guide to Planning for the Future of Your Farm*. Washington, DC: American Farmland Trust, 2002. First published in 1997.

Covert, John. *Keeping the Family in the Family Ranch: Traditional Values, New Perspectives*. Arvada, CO: Colorado Cattlemen's Agricultural Land Trust, 1997.

Diehl, Janet and Thomas S. Barrett. *The Conservation Easement Handbook*. Washington, DC: Trust for Public Land and the Land Trust Alliance, 1988.

Gustanski, Julie Ann and Roderick H. Squires, eds. *Protecting the Land: Conservation Easements Past, Present, and Future*. Washington, DC: Island Press, 2000.

Knight, Richard L., Wendell C. Gilgert and Ed Marston, eds. *Ranching West of the 100th Meridian: Culture, Ecology, Economics*. Washington, DC: Island Press, 2002.

Leopold, Aldo. *A Sand County Almanac*. New York: Ballantine Books, 1970. First published in 1949.

Lind, Brenda and Marty Zeller. *Working Ranchland Conservation Easements: Results from the Working Ranchland Conservation Easement Learning Circle, Sundance, UT 2001*. Washington, DC: Land Trust Alliance, 2002.

McHarg, Ian L. *Design with Nature*. New York: John Wiley & Sons, 1992. First published in 1971.

Nagel, Stefan, et al. *Appraising Easements*. Washington, DC: Land Trust Alliance and the National Trust for Historic Preservation, 2003. First published in 1984.

Rosan, Liz, ed. *Preserving Working Ranches in the West*. Tucson, AZ: The Sonoran Institute, 2001.

Small, Stephen J. *Preserving Family Lands: Book I*. Boston, MA: Landowner Planning Center, 1998. First published in 1988.

Small, Stephen J. *Preserving Family Lands: Book II*. Boston, MA: Landowner Planning Center, 1997.

Small, Stephen J. *Preserving Family Lands: Book III*. Boston, MA: Landowner Planning Center, 2002.

Veslany, Kathleen, ed. *Purchasing Development Rights: Conserving Land, Preserving Western Livelihoods*. Denver, CO: Western Governor's Association; San Francisco, CA: The Trust for Public Land; and Washington, DC: National Cattlemen's Beef Association, 2002.

About the Authors

Anthony Anella

Born and raised in Albuquerque, Anthony Anella spent his early summers working on farms and ranches in New Mexico. From that experience he gained an abiding respect for the land and the people who earn their living on the land. He is the principal of Anthony Anella Architect AIA (anella.com), an Albuquerque practice dedicated to site-sensitive design. He is also a partner in Conservation Design Partners (conservationdesign.net), an Albuquerque-based group that specializes in conservation easement design and development. He believes that good design is distinguished by the art of listening and by letting the land do most of the talking.

John B. Wright

"Jack" has twenty-eight years of experience designing conservation easements on ranches. He has been involved with more than 114 easement projects across the American West. During the early 1970s, Jack was a land use planning director in a rural Montana county where he saw the tough choices ranchers have to make. He earned his Ph.D. in Geography from UC Berkeley in 1990 and is a professor of geography at New Mexico State University. Jack divides his time between New Mexico and Montana and all the ranchlands in between.

Edward Ranney

Edward Ranney is an internationally recognized landscape photographer. His work is included in the permanent collections of the Art Institute of Chicago, the Museum of Modern Art in New York, and other museums in this country and abroad. A resident of Santa Fe, New Mexico, his work has also been published in *Monuments of the Incas, Stonework of the Maya,* and *Prairie Passage.*

Index

A
access, public, 15, 32, 66, 109
accounting fees, 35
advisers, selection of, 20, 41–43, 49
agricultural land, prime, 72–75, 74, *f6.4*
agricultural practices, new, 33
annual monitoring visits, 46, 109, 128, 137–38
appraisals
    "before" and "after," 26
    costs, 35
    definition, 43–44
    overaggressive, 27
    preliminary, 27, **44**, 91
    process of conducting, 26–27
    "shelf life" of final, 27, 91
    valuation of property rights, 98–99
appraisers, selection of, 43–44, 99
arbitrary restrictions, avoidance of, 86
archaeological sites, 23, 75, 76, *f6.5*, 127, *f9.7*
Arendt, Randall G., 70
attorneys, selection of, 42–43
audits, 43

B
Barbour, Cora, 114
baseline reports
    conservation value of land, 55
    cost of, 35
    functions of, 21, 23–24, 52, 109, 138
    geology and landforms in, 55
    graphic materials in, 45
    historic values in, 56, 58
    hydrology, 55
    natural resource inventories compared to, 53–54
    open spaces in, 56–57
    owner acknowledgment statement in, 54
    preparation of, 21–24, 52–53
    vegetation in, 55
biocide use, 66
Blackfoot River Valley, 107, 113–14
Blackwood Ranch, 114
"blowsand" zones, 127, *f9.9*
Breakell, Burgess v. (1995), 139
buildable land, house sites relative to, 75, 78, *f6.9—10*, 129, *f9.12*
building envelopes, 27, 80, 101, 125
buildings and structures, 63, 128
Burgess v. Breakell (1995), 139

C
capital gains, 101
Carrie Hilger Ranch, 112
"carryforward" rule, 91
carrying capacity, 86
case studies

Blackfoot River Valley, 113–14
Hilger Hereford Ranch, 110–12
Montosa Ranch, 115–35
types of, 107–8
"Woods Ranch," 108–9
CCALT. *See* Colorado Cattlemen's Agricultural Land Trust (CCALT)
CC&Rs. *See* Covenants, Conditions, and Restrictions (CC&Rs)
charitable deduction examples, 101–2
Colorado Cattlemen's Agricultural Land Trust (CCALT), 20, 46
commercial gravel pits, 109
commercial uses, 65
commodities, nontraditional, 98
common law, English, 17
comparable sales identification, 44
condemnation, 38
conflict avoidance, 85–86
conservation
    areas, 71–72, 78, f6.8, 129, f9.11
    buyers, 3, 35, 48
    economics of, 3, 81
    qualified contributions, 22
Conservation Design for Subdivisions (Arendt), 70
Conservation Design Partners, 119
conservation development
    advantages of, 97
    balance in, 85, f7.1
    case studies, 108, 115–35
    compromises required, 85
    conventional development *vs.*, 80–81
    decision benchmarks, 92–93
    developers and, 48
    land ownership in, 80, f6.12
    marketing of, 49, 89–90
    preventing further subdivision in, 90
    scenarios for, 119–22
    value creation in, 83–85
conservation easement deeds
    in hierarchy of restrictions, 89
    as instrument of record, 52
    model language, 147–61
    parts of, 61–62
    restrictions included, 15, 25, 32, 62, 67
conservation easements
    amendments to, 61
    choices in, 7–10
    design of, 12, 61–68
    donation of, 30, 35, 37, 125
    enforcement of, 28, 34, 36, 46, 89, 138–42
    enhancement value of, 26–27, 70–71, 98–99, 101, 125
    exclusions from, 62–63, 98–99, 101
    extinguishment of, 37, 61
    financial advantages of, 97–106
    free enterprise and, 38
    history of, 17–18
    language in, 85–86, 139, 147–61
    models for, 42, 142, 147–61
    negotiation of, 61, 88–89
    as "non-possessory interest," 38
    opposition and support for, 30–31
    process for completion of, 20–30
    qualification criteria, 31
    receivers of, 16, 33–34 (*see also* land trusts)
    recording of, 28, 91, 100
    restrictions included, 25
    restrictions on, 15, 32, 62, 67
    review by land trust board, 27–28

scenarios for, 119–10, 122–23
tax benefits, 100–102
typical elements included, 109, *f9.2*
variations in, 108, *f9.1*
violations of, 33, 36, 138–39
conservation land planners, selection of, 44–45
conservation organizations, qualified, 99
 See also land trusts
conservation purposes qualification, 22–23, 37
conservation value of land
 in baseline report, 55
 as commodity, 9
 federal tax laws and, 99
 over time, 2–3
 protection of, 89
 qualitative land analysis and, 69
consistent land uses, 62
contributions
 endowment/stewardship, 28, 35, 89, 128
 qualified conservation, 22
 See also conservation easements, donation of
conventional development
 conservation developments *vs.*, 80–81
 description of, 10–13
 land ownership in, 81, *f6.13*
 quantitative land analysis and, 69
cooperation, regional, 107
Covenants, Conditions, and Restrictions (CC&Rs), 87
 See also restrictive covenants
Cox, Billie, xi, 116
Cox, B.W., xi, 1, 116–17, *116p*

D
decision-making
 about conservation development, 92–93
 about conservation easements, 49
 decision tree, 7, 8, *f1.2*, 9
deed restrictions *vs.*. easements, 36
 See also restrictive covenants
deeds of conservation easement
 in hierarchy of restrictions, 89
 as instrument of record, 52
 model language, 147–61
 parts of, 61–62
 restrictions included, 15, 25, 32, 62, 67
Depression, Great, 111
Design with Nature (McHarg), 70
developers, real estate, 47–48, 69
development
 conventional, 10–13, 69, 80–81, 81, *f6.13*
 limited, 9, 12–13, 24–25
 minimizing impact of, 83–85
 rights, 9, 15, 36–37, 98, 103 (*see also* property rights)
 See also conservation development
diagrams, use in analysis, 77
documentation, photographic, 57, 77, 139
donation of conservation easements
 cost of, 35
 criteria for qualification, 31
 process of, 28
 reasons for, 30, 37
 value of, 98–99, 125
drainage, natural, 126, *f9.4*

E

easements
   term, 31
   zoning regulations *vs.*, 36
   deed restrictions *vs.*, 36
   See also conservation easements; restrictive covenants
Economic Growth and Tax Relief Reconciliation Act of 2001, 103–4
economics of conservation, 3, 81
Eder, Jenny and Otto, 114
elk habitat, 127, f9.8
endowment contributions, 28, 35, 89, 128
enforcement of conservation easements, 28, 34, 36, 46, 89, 138–42
English common law, 17
enhancement value
   of conservation easements, 26–27, 70–71, 98–99, 101, 124
   of open spaces, 69, 70–71
envelopes, building, 27, 80, 101, 125
estate taxes, 7, 10, 45, 100, 102–5
exclusions from conservation easements, 62–63, 98–99, 101
extent of use, 30
extinguishment of conservation easements, 37, 61

F

facts *vs.* rumors, 38–39
fair market value (FMV), 26, 123
federal tax laws, 99–100
fees, legal and accounting, 35
fee simple title, 16, 80, 97
fieldwork, 53
50 percent limitation on tax deduction, 100
financial advantages of conservation easements, 97–106
financial advisers, selection of, 42–43
financial reserves, 109

5 Star Double R Ranch, 114
Five Valleys Land Trust, 115
FMV. *See* fair market value (FMV)
forest management plans, 65
free enterprise and conservation easements, 38
future innovations, allowances for, 33
future land uses, 62–67

G

garbage storage or disposal, 66
gas wells, 64
Gates of the Mountains, 110–11
geologists, roles and responsibilities, 24, 52, 57
geology and landforms in baseline report, 55
gift value, 98–99, 124
government involvement, 37–38
graphic materials in baseline report, 45
gravel pits, commercial, 109
grazing, 1, 33, 64–65, 109
Great Depression, 111

H

habitat protection, 22, 56, 74, f6.3, 127, f9.8
Hauser Dam, 111
herbicide use, 66
Herefords, Polled, 111
Hilger, Nicholas, 110–11
Hilger Hereford Ranch, 110–12
historic preservation, 15, 23
historic sites, 75, 76, f6.5
historic values in baseline report, 56, 58
Homeowner's Associations and bylaws, 67, 87
house sites

analysis of, 78–79, *f6.11*, 125, 132–135, *f9.15—19*
relative to buildable land, 75, 78, *f6.9—10*, 129, *f9.12*
relative to viewshed, 131, *f9.14*
hydrology in baseline report, 55

I

income generation projects, 24–25
income tax benefits, 10, 100–102
inconsistent land uses, 62
industrial/commercial uses, 65
infrastructure, 129, *f9.13*
innovations, allowances for future, 33
Internal Revenue Code, 17, 102–3
Internal Revenue Service audits, 43
inventories, 45, 53–54

K

keeping the ranch, threats to, 1–2, 7
keep the ranch *vs.* sell the ranch, 6, *f1.1*

L

Lake Valley Ranch photographs, *50p, 82p, 94—6p, 140—41p, 144p*
land
  analysis of, 69
  buildable, 75, 78, *f6.9—10*, 129, *f9.12*
  preservation of, 70–71
  prime agricultural, 72–75, 74, f6.4
  protection of, 83–85, 84
land development
  assessment of need for, 24–25
  conservation *vs.* conventional, 80–81
  conventional, 10–13, 69, 80–81, *f6.13*
  land protection balance and, 84
  minimizing impact of, 83–85
land management, 54–55
  See also forest management plans; grazing; ranch management; recreation management agreements; timber management
landowners, 15, 16, 30, 87–89
landscape analysis, 51, 77, 78–79, *f6.11—12*
Land Trust Alliance, 33, 47, 146
land trusts
  conservation easements and, 15–16, 18–20, 27–28
  contact information for, 46–47
  definition and missions of, 17–18
  interests of *vs.*. landowner interests, 87–89
  roles and responsibilities of, 35, 44, 46, 87–88, 137
  "rule against perpetuities" and, 37
  selection of, 20, 45–46
  See also conservation easements, receivers of
land uses
  consistent with easement, 62
  future, 62–67
  management of, 54–55
  planning regulations *vs.* easements, 36
  restrictions on, 25
  See also property rights
land valuations
  changes over time, 2–3
  for conservation, 9, 55, 69, 84, 89
  for development, 9
  for estate tax purposes, 102
  federal tax laws and, 99
language
  in baseline report, 24
  in conservation easements, 85–86, 139, 147–61
legal advisers, selection of, 42–43

legal fees, 35
legends, rural, 38
lenders, 34
Lewis, Meriwether, 110
liens, subordination of, 21
life estates, 112
limited development, 9, 12–13, 24–25
   See also conservation development
Lindbergh, Land, 114
livestock management, 1, 33, 64–65, 109
loans, 34
lot lines, 80, 129, *f9.13*
lot ownership deed, 89
Lunn v. the Tokekeke Association (1992), 139

M

management plans and agreements, 66, 86, 114
maps, 45, 57, 72–75
   See also individual map layers
McHarg, Ian, 70
mineral rights, 24, 32, 63–64
model conservation easements, 42, 142, 147–61
monitoring visits, 46, 109, 128, 137–38
Montana Land Reliance, 18, 112, 115
Montosa Ranch, 108, 115–35, 115, *f9.3*
   photographs, 14p, 19p, 29p, 40p, 59p—60p, 68p, 106p, 117p, 125p, 136p, 162p
Monture Hereford Ranch, 114

N

National Cattlemen's Beef Association, 20
natural drainage, 126, *f9.4*
Natural Heritage Program, 53
natural resource inventories, 53–54

The Nature Conservancy, 115
negotiation of easements, 61, 88–89
New Mexico Land Conservation Collaborative (NMLCC), 128
nonbuildable peaks, 72, 73, *f6.1*, 126, *f9.5*
nontraditional commodities, 98

O

oil wells, 64
Olmsted, Frederick Law, Jr., 70
The Open Lands Demonstration Project, xi
open spaces
   in baseline report, 56–57
   development advantages of, 80–81
   enhancement value of, 69, 70–71
   preservation of, 15, 22–23, 84, 99
opposition to conservation easements, 31
organizations, qualified conservation, 99
   See also land trusts
owner acknowledgment statement in baseline report, 54
ownership succession, 34, 87, 104

P

PDR. See Purchase of Development Rights (PDR)
peaks, nonbuildable, 72, 73, *f6.1*, 126, *f9.5*
"performance clauses," 86
pesticide use, 66
photo documentation, 57, 77, 139
physical description in baseline report, 55
plain language in conservation easements, 85–86, 139, 147–61
Plains of San Agustín, 115
planners, conservation land, 44–45
Polled Herefords, 111
predator control, 66

prime agricultural land, 72–75, f6.4
private property rights. *See* property rights
process for completing conservation easement, 20–30
professional advice, 41–50, 105
professional advisers, selection of, 20, 41–43, 49
project scope, 51
property rights
   development, 15, 36–37, 98, 103
   mineral, 24, 32, 63–64
   respect for, 5, 16
   valuation of, 98–99
   water, 32, 64
property taxes, 35, 105
public access, 15, 32, 66, 109
public viewsheds, 75, 77, f6.7, 131, f9.14
purchase of development rights (PDR), 9, 36–37
"purposes clause," 86

Q

qualification categories of "conservation purposes," 22–23
qualified conservation organizations, 99
   See also land trusts
qualitative land analysis and sieve mapping, 69
quantitative land analysis and conventional development, 69
questions and answers, 30–39
questions to consider, 5, 7, 92–93, 97
quid pro quo, disallowance of, 90

R

ranch easements, basic, 107, 108–12
ranchers as land stewards, 137
ranching, threats to, 1–2, 7, 145
ranch management, 33, 87, 109

ranch ownership deed, 89
real estate brokers, 49
real estate developers, 47–48, 69
real estate values, 89
"reasonable person" criterion, 86
recording of conservation easements, 28, 91, 100
recreational uses, 22, 65–66, 103
recreation management agreements, 66, 114
regional cooperation, 107, 113–15
remoteness test and mineral rights, 24
reserves, financial, 109
restrictions, easement
   on buildings and structures, 128
   examples of, 109
   hierarchy of, 89
   language of, 85–87
   negotiation of, 88–89
restrictive covenants, 36, 67, 87–91, 123
road layout and design, 64, 77
The Rose of Helena, 111
"rule against perpetuities," 37
rumors *vs.* facts, 38–39
rural legends, 38

S

scenarios for conservation easements, 119–10, 122–23
scenic easements, 15
scope of project, 51
sell the ranch *vs.* keep the ranch, 6, f1.1
Sheftl v. Lebel (1998), 139
SHPO. *See* State Historic Preservation Office (SHPO)
sieve mapping
   cost of, 35

definition of, 69–70
as design process, 81
examples of, 75–83
history of, 70–71
six-year "carryforward" rule, 100, 102
slopes, steep, 75, 76, *f6.6*, 128, *f9.10*
species lists, 57
State Historic Preservation Office (SHPO), 52–53
Steele, Fanny, 114
steep slopes, 75, 76, *f6.6*, 128, *f9.10*
steps for completing conservation easement, 20–30
stewardship
    about, 137–44
    conservation easements as reward for, 10
    endowments for, 28, 35, 89, 128
    formalizing, 3
    importance to ranchers, 1
stream channel alteration, 64
structures and buildings, 63, 128
subdivision, 62–63, 67, 80, 90, 130
subordination of lien, 21
succession of ownership, 34, 87, 104
summary information in baseline report, 54
supporters of conservation easements, 30
surface mining, restrictions on, 63–64

T
takedowns, 26
Taos Land Trust, 18
taxes
    benefits of conservation easements, 10, 46, 100–102
    Economic Growth and Tax Relief Reconciliation Act of 2001, 103–4
    estate, 7, 10, 45, 100, 102–5
    evaluation of potential benefits, 91
    federal laws, 99–100
    Internal Revenue Code, 17, 102–3
    Internal Revenue Service audits, 43
    laws governing benefits, 84, 99–100
    property, 35, 105
    term requirements for deductions, 31
Taxpayer Relief Act of 1997, 104
Tax Reform Act of 1976, 17
Tax Treatment Extension Act of 1980, 17
term easements, 31
term requirements for tax deductions, 31
terms of art, 86
third party intrusions, 34
30 percent limitation on tax deduction, 100
timber management, 65
tipping point, 5, 6, *f1.1*
title report, 21
titles, fee simple, 16, 80, 97
Tokekeke Association, Lunn v. the (1992), 139
trash storage or disposal, 66
Trinchera Ranch, 11–12

U
Uniform Conservation Easement Act of 1981, 17

V
value, enhancement
    of conservation easements, 26–27, 70–71, 98–99, 101, 124
    of open spaces, 69, 70–71
vegetation in baseline report, 55
viewsheds, public, 75, 77, f6.7, 131, *f9.14*
violations of conservation easements, 28, 33, 36, 138–39

W
water bodies and drainage, 72, 73, *f6.2*
water lines and wells, 126, *f9.6*
water rights, 32, 64
wells, oil and gas, 64
"whereas" statements, 62, 139
Whidbey-Camano Land Trust, 139
Wild Horse Ranch, 12
wildlife and wildlife habitat, 56, 74, f6.3
"Woods Ranch" case study, 108–9
Wyoming as exception, 17

Z
zoning regulations *vs.* easements, 36

Island Press Board of Directors

Victor M. Sher, Esq. *(Chair)*
Sher & Leff
San Francisco, CA

Dane A. Nichols *(Vice-Chair)*
Washington, DC

Carolyn Peachey *(Secretary)*
Campbell, Peachey & Associates
Washington, DC

Drummond Pike *(Treasurer)*
President
The Tides Foundation
San Francisco, CA

Robert E. Baensch
Director, Center for Publishing
New York University
New York, NY

David C. Cole
President
Aquaterra, Inc.
Washington, VA

Catherine M. Conover
Quercus LLC
Washington, DC

William H. Meadows
President
The Wilderness Society
Washington, DC

Henry Reath
Collectors Reprints
Princeton, NJ

Will Rogers
President
The Trust for Public Land
San Francisco, CA

Charles C. Savitt
President
Island Press
Washington, DC

Susan E. Sechler
Senior Advisor
The German Marshall Fund
Washington, DC

Peter R. Stein
General Partner
LTC Conservation Advisory Services
The Lyme Timber Company
Hanover, NH

Diana Wall, Ph.D.
Director and Professor
Natural Resource Ecology Laboratory
Colorado State University
Fort Collins, CO

Wren Wirth
Washington, DC